ANTONIO
GUIDA

Paris

Zurich

Milan

Florence

Porto Ercole

Rome

Campania

Apulia

This book was born from the meeting of Antonio Guida, with Giacomo Bretzel and Maddalena Fossati a sunny morning in Tuscany.

To Michelina

COOKING WITH
ANTONIO GUIDA

Photos by **Giacomo Bretzel**
Texts by **Maddalena Fossati**

SilvanaEditoriale

Contents

All the temperatures in the recipes are expressed in degrees Celsius

Introduction

I spent a week in Antonio Guida's kitchen at the Mandarin Oriental Hotel in Milan. Watching, immobile, concerned that I would disturb the team's frenetic activity and throw off their clockwork precision where burners in action not only raised the level of unpredictability but also the ambient temperature. A performance repeated every evening where the kitchen becomes a theater, with all the energy of opening night.

Beginning of dinner service. It starts: the order arrives and for a precise instant, perceptible in the air, everyone stops as if there were some magic switch. The chef repeats the order out loud so that every member of the team, from the station chefs to the apprentices, can hear. He is answered by a compact baritonal chorus of "yes chef"'s because the conductor must be sure that everyone has understood. And immediately, things begin to move once again: people busy cooking meat, fish, completing a first course or placing a dish on the pass. A perfectly-honed machine capable of continuously managing the unexpected.

The serving staff enters and exits through the automatic doors, first to place the orders, then to leave with food-laden trays. All the young men and women have the concentrated expression of those who strive for perfection. Careful not to let the liquid in the plates quiver, their muscles are tense, slightly trembling, their expressions those of people who know they are doing something important. In total complicity with those in the kitchen. The alchemy of ingredients that become dishes flows uninterruptedly, like electrical current, from the burners to the tables of the restaurant; the cooperation is intense and absolute.

And once the predictable is under control, the unexpected occurs. In the dining room and it can't be controlled, it's part of the unpredictable world of the restaurant. A woman is allergic, six diners go out for a smoke as their orders are ready. In this ever-changing picture, Antonio Guida is there, unflappable. Calm expression. Sometimes at the service pass, or looking at the team—the group as a whole and every single area of the kitchen. He moves from the first courses to the meats; he stops at the saucier, handling a bit of uncertainty and effort calmly and respectfully. The cooks prepare, handle and touch each ingredient with meticulous delicacy, just the way the master chef taught them. Nothing ostentatious, just the desire to respect the raw materials and follow the recipe precisely. They work feverishly. The waitstaff is back. One person slices the bread, another fills the bread baskets with the grissini made with loving care that afternoon. In the meantime, snow-white porcelain dishes come and go under the lights, the setting for something intense and powerful—the flavors that Antonio Guida studies, creates and invents every week, every day... non-stop. That's who Antonio is, a calm man and profoundly passionate about flavors. "I became a cook because I'm a glutton" and this book tells his story, through his signature dishes, the ingredients, the emotions—from Apulia and his family's vegetable garden, to Milan, with stops along the way in Paris, Zurich and even Alaska.

Maddalena Fossati

A man, a chef

"I have met extremely generous people along the way. In the kitchen and pastry lab I always felt at home."

"I grew up in a home with a vegetable garden that had everything. Today, we would call it synergy. It seemed to be one big mess, but in that chaos, the lemon-balm grew next to the strawberries, the basil next to the zucchinis and everything—all the vegetables and all the fruit—grew and thrived, together. My parents, Michelina and Donato, have always been passionate about food. From the time I was small, we planted eggplant, peppers, tomatoes and potatoes, and we lived off what we produced. Even today, when my father offers you a slice of melon, he'll get up and pick it directly from the garden, even if now, given his age, he doesn't spend that much time there. I remember clearly the unadulterated flavor of food. We also raised pigs, rabbits and guinea hens, just for us, and the only things we had to buy were lamb, beef and, of course, fish. Then my mother would work her magic, charming an ever-changing number of people at the table. Sundays there were always at least ten or twelve guests, but that was the moment when all her creative juices flowed and she always succeeded in making everyone happy. We kids had our own tasks, each assigned by the chef who, sweetly but firmly, explained what we were to do. It became a rite: washing hands, putting on the hair cap, lighting the wood stove, the handmade pasta. I was assigned to the bread, from the dough to the baking, and I also had to deal with the sauces and seasonings. Sundays in the summer were spent in the countryside, which was actually less than a mile from home, but it seemed like a real outing. With Aunt Cesarea, my grandmother Assunta's sister, and her husband Angiolino, we started cooking at dawn. Around noon my fantastic four cousins arrived, including Filippo, with whom I always went fishing, Patrizia, Maria Domenica and Cosimina, as well as many other relatives, and when we sat down at the table, there were always at least twenty of us! My aunt was like my second mother and we spent a lot of time together. They were magical moments that I still recall with tremendous nostalgia—precious instants from my past." This is Antonio Guida, a man who, in his starred kitchen, talks about his family with the same simplicity he used to light the oven when a boy. And this is the source of the flavors in his cuisine. This is the source of his desire to feed us well, to make us happy with each bite, at Seta just like at home where on Sundays he prepares his famed lamb and his sagne pasta, just the way his mother Michelina did. "Just think, my mother was always a very creative cook. Many times she changed the recipe as she went along. She never stopped. I only ever saw one other person important in my life do this: Pierre Gagnaire!"

After the Sundays with his aunt, Antonio's career continued at the hotel and catering vocational school in Santa Cesarea. "My father did not have much faith in my academic future since I had never done well in school, but there, I put my heart into it and I worked hard and became good. At home they couldn't believe it. Mom came back from the meetings with the teachers humming to herself, absolutely amazed. After years of mediocre grades, I had become a first-rate student. Our kitchen at home became my laboratory with the pantry and chest of drawers for every type of pasta, taken from the old general store my grandmother Ermelinda, my father's mother, had in town. I realized very young

Antonio in front of the church of San Domenico at Tricase

what I wanted to do. With my friend Romano, we had everything planned. At the time, he was a waiter in a restaurant and we dreamed of opening a place together. We took notes about where we wanted to visit, where we wanted to work. Recently, in my home in Orbetello, I found the notebook where I had written out our plan, down to the last detail! I wanted to go to a French hotel and catering school because that was the top. I dreamed about going to France. And when Alain Ducasse began to take off, I found my idol. I fantasized about traveling to Mexico and South America. But top of the list was Switzerland where I wanted to study to be a maître chocolatier. While I was at cooking school, I had worked in the shop of Rafelino Bello in Galatina and Torre dell'Orso (in the province of Lecce), and Switzerland seemed to me to be the best place to follow in the footsteps of my teacher. He had also been to Queen Elizabeth II at Buckingham Palace, and in the 1950s he returned home to Apulia in a Rolls Royce." A man who taught Antonio the foundations, first and foremost, and passed on to him values that were important. "Meeting the right people has a tremendous effect on our future and Rafelino opened the way for me, he got me on track." Like a prophet inspires a disciple, or the way Virgil led Dante out of Inferno, Rafelino guided Antonio through the excesses of adolescence. "He taught me discipline and to respect the product, the importance of wasting nothing and bringing out the best in every ingredient. And patience. Like many young people, I wanted everything, immediately, and it was hard for me to understand. He was able to share his knowledge with me little by little. Before introducing me to any recipe, he showed me how to move around a pastry shop. 'Just watch,' he said, 'before showing you how to temper chocolate or how to make short crust dough, you have to learn how to move, how to be part of a team. In a group, the most important thing is being in tune with each other. When you're not, the whole machine jams.'

Michelina, Antonio's mother

Donato, Antonio's father

I started by washing dishes. In a pastry shop, you don't have someone who washes the dishes, you have to do it yourself. 'Before teaching you how to make custard or dough, you have to know your products. Do you know how to wash a pan? No? Well, learn, then we'll see.' He was hard on me, but it made me appreciate the recipe more. If someone just gives you something without having to work for it, you don't appreciate its full worth. If, however, you attain it gradually, you treasure that gift. It took me eight months, maybe a year, to 'earn' short crust pastry. And even then, Rafelino only revealed half of what he knew. A way of thinking and acting that I found in Tokyo when, many years later, I spent a few months in Roppongi. A respect for wisdom, for experience and for age."

At a certain point, I left "It was the first big adventure of my life, that cruise ship. The opportunity was given me by Cosimo Pantaleo, a chef my parents knew in town and who had worked on the Raffaello cruise ship. He was an important person in my growth. I met him in Lecce and he told me all about life on-board and the number of Italians who worked on the ship. And he urged me to see the world, to not stay in Salento.
I set off very early one morning, my mother puttering around the kitchen, sad and crying in fits and starts, for once unsure about what to do. I had to leave, to get away. My cousin Maria Domenica had come to pick me up and take me to the train station. Dawn had just broken and I left Depressa as the town was still sleeping. And I took the first flight of my life, from Rome. The first stopover was in Zurich, with Vancouver as the final destination. I didn't speak a word of English and I suffered from seasickness. I told myself: you'll get used to it. I landed in Amsterdam where I was to get the intercontinental flight and where there were other young people who were supposed to embark with me. A traveling companion convinced me to go bar-hopping. All of sudden, the world opened up before my eyes. Night spots, bars ... I had never seen anything like it. It was all so different from Depressa. I was totally dazed by all the lights in the Dutch capital.

On-board my first ship, I was happy and relieved because I thought the seasickness had left me. Then I realized that I felt good because we were still in port. I was 19. I didn't know anything, I hadn't seen the world. Luckily, ours was a 3-month itinerary from Vancouver with a number of stopovers in Alaska, and going through the fjords, the sea was fairly calm.

Every day I discovered something new. I was always afraid I'd make some mistake. I wanted to show myself and others that I could do it. I was the first to start and the last to finish. Life on the ship was tough. We started at seven in the morning and worked until eleven at night, with a half-day off every two weeks. Then we changed route towards the Caribbean and my seasickness problem hit with a bang. I really suffered. I tried band-aids, bracelets, gum. I ate salty anchovies, worked both standing and sitting... nothing helped the nausea and vomiting. Each time every two weeks, I just collapsed. In the meantime, I advanced in the kitchen and moved up to the sauces. I had to stick it out for six months to keep my contract, and I did. Then I left".

The years in Zurich "They were great. After a time at home I found a job at the Savoy Hotel and hooked up again with my friend Romano who, in the meantime, had gone to live in Switzerland. He had given up his dreams, but we saw a lot of each other and we hung out, drinking and eating. Plus, in the kitchen, I encountered everything I had studied at school. I liked the highly-organized environment and in the restaurant, I was assigned to first courses. Time passed and I had a girlfriend in town who continued to ask me: 'when are you coming back?'. To tell the truth, I had no intention of returning. The choice was going to Depressa and getting married, or France. I wanted France. I sent a number of resumés to leading French chefs with two or three Michelin stars in Paris and London. In the hotel there was a girl from Algeria who helped me write a cover letter which, apparently, Pierre Gagnaire liked very much and he called me immediately. Later he told me that what I had written made an impression on him. Guy Savoy and the London Savoy also responded".

You start Monday "I arrived in Paris in November, if I remember correctly, it was November 7, 1996. In front of the restaurant in Rue Balzac there were stacks of cartons filled with food and bottles of wine ready to be taken into the restaurant. Instinctively, I began to help and immediately after I met Pierre Gagnaire. I entered his restaurant. It was the great French restaurant. An institution, a holy place that instilled dread and respect, joy and fear. It was the place I had dreamed of while at school, during the summers in Depressa and those months of seasickness in the ship kitchen. My dream was coming true and, in fact, my interview with Monsieur lasted just two minutes, and he said: 'You start Monday'.

I panicked, also because it was Friday and I hadn't expected everything to happen so quickly. I had already rented a small studio apartment in Place des Vosges, but it was completely empty! During the next two days I furnished my little abode as best as I could and then I presented myself at the restaurant. Those first nights I hardly slept: I was so excited by what I was seeing every day in the kitchen.

The team was fantastic, unified. My dream was coming true. The chef was very creative and continuously changed the dishes. His kitchen was very dynamic. He would even change a sauce or how a dish was to be presented during service if he liked it better. An important lesson I learned from that French chef who taught me to think outside the box and never rest on my laurels. And he taught me the concept of harmony between flavors, a sense of elegance—aspects to always strive for in a dish.

Thanks to him, I learned how to dare successfully with different combinations and plating. Many in the kitchen thought we already knew each other because we immediately found we

Antonio in the alleys of Tricase

DEL
MEZZOGIORNO

were on the same wavelength. Monsieur Gagnaire is a very friendly person who likes to work as a group. He listens and teaches a lot, including interpersonal relations.
Plus, there was Paris. Simply splendid. In two years I was promoted from apprentice to assistant to station chef. I was responsible for a strategic part of the restaurant and lots of things happened. I even cooked for President Chirac when the chef was invited to the Elysée. The menu included suckling pig with mace (covering of the nutmeg seed) and a chocolate and pumpkin dessert. During the afternoon, I didn't take a single break, I wanted to learn as much as possible. I went into the pastry lab to help the pastry chefs who taught me their techniques and tricks. I lent a hand to the assistants to try to understand as much as possible because the pastry team was also very strong and creative. They used daring combinations and very little sugar. I tasted beer gelato which, at the time, was very innovative. I was one of the few on the team that knew everything that happened in the kitchen. For the first time, I learned how to make chocolates using a two- or three-pronged fork, without a mold. And I made a lot of friends. There were nine of us in the kitchen, plus 4 on the pastry team. We began at 8 am and finished at midnight. Saturdays we would go out for a beer. Hervé was the junior sous chef and we always worked together. We are still very good friends. He taught me a lot. Even after my time with Gagnaire, every year I returned to visit him in his home in Paris and vice versa. The same with the pastry sous chef Richard who asked me to be the godfather of his son Pierre (named after Gagnaire).
I have met extremely generous people along the way. In the kitchen and pastry lab I always felt at home. When you work together so closely, you help each other, at least that's what I've experienced. We supported each other."

Boats in the port of Tricase

Antonio with friends, including his dear one Rosanna

The Getaway "I literally ran away from Paris because things were good, too good. I was so happy that I was afraid I would just remain blocked there. My idea was to do something nice in Italy. In my childhood plan, I wanted to return home and I was getting too comfortable in the French capital. Sundays I spent with friends and colleagues and I had a French girlfriend. The decision was difficult to make, but I worked out my departure with the chef, giving 4 months' notice, and then I left. But before I left, I introduced him to another Italian: Stefano Baiocco. Baiocco worked for Ducasse, at the Louis XV.

It was an encounter for life. In one of my trips back to Italy, at the airport, I became friends with a guy who knew Stefano. We exchanged phone numbers and, one day, while I was in Gagnaire's kitchen, he said there was a call for me. It was Stefano who said he wanted to work in Rue Balzac. At the beginning, he just wanted some extra hours, and that wasn't possible, but we agreed that I would introduce him to the chef. The moment was perfect because I was getting ready to return to Italy.

We met for the first time one spring morning at the Saint Paul metro stop, in front of the carousel, and we recognized each other immediately. Selfies and social networks didn't exist at the time, it was just instinct. Without even Google Images to help us, we said hello and immediately became great friends. We saw each other in Paris and then Stefano and his then-girlfriend but now-wife Olga came to visit me in Apulia. My mother was happy, exactly like those Sundays in which the kitchen and the whole scene were hers, and we all cooked up a storm. My dream after that vacation was to open a restaurant together: me, Stefano, Mom. What a trio that would have been.

Antonio with his wife Luciana, his friends Rosanna and Tommaso during an aperitif by the sea in the port of Tricase

When we got back from the discotheque, she would have home-baked bread just out of the oven waiting for us. My brothers were away, so Mom was all ours. Every day was a holiday and Stefano gained over 20 pounds of flesh and happiness in a week! In September, thanks to him, I started at the Enoteca Pinchiorri."

Then Florence "The year was 1999 and I went to work for Madame Féolde and Giorgio Pinchiorri as station chef. It was the temple of restaurants and they had, and still have, one of the best wine cellars in the world. I liked working for them. A nice, positive year of new discoveries, in which the regional cuisine was offered simply, but sublimely. The pici all'agliona (thick spaghetti with garlic tomato sauce) with toasted herb bread, and pigeon with beans are dishes that will remain in my memory and on my palate forever. Then I headed south, because I wanted to get closer to my home, both geographically and in terms of cuisine. So, I found a job at Don Alfonso. It reminded me of my childhood, with the ingredients that arrived daily from Punta Campanella, their fantastic garden. I stayed a year."

Luciana "In July 2000, before going to Rome, I moved for three months to a friend's hotel in Jesolo. He was in trouble and asked me to help him. Luciana worked in the same hotel as a housekeeper. For me, it was love at first sight. But not for her. The first time I saw her was in the kitchen. Her eyes sparkled. Her smile lit up the room. Amazing spirit and incredible energy. I fell in love with her immediately. I prepared a bag lunch for her and her colleagues, and each time I created something special for her. I tried to win her over using what I knew best. Pasta and rice salads filled with fresh herbs, and petits fours with carefully-arranged fresh fruit on top. On our first date, we went to see an exhibit of Kandinsky prints, the only alternative to a stroll through town. She was very busy because during the day she worked in the hotel and in the evening she studied sociology at La Sapienza university. At a certain point, she returned to Rome and I followed her. I found a job in the capital, at the Eden Hotel. For the first time, love for a woman gained precedence over my professional choices. I could either be with Luciana, or go to London. This time, I chose Luciana. Not that there was anything wrong with the Eden, quite the contrary. It was just that Rome was not on my famous list. We got an apartment together, near the central train station, in Via Goito, and in the afternoons, we took walks throughout the city. I cooked spaghetti with tomato sauce for her, a dish she loved."

15 months "I spent just over a year in the capital and worked for Enrico Derflingher as station chef and then junior sous chef. And I met Federico Dell'Omarino who was first course station chef. We became friends immediately. He was so alert and active... A real volcano! Rome was important, a cross-roads in my destined path because in addition to Fede, I also met Gianfranco. He was the man who brought us truffles and often stayed to eat with us. He was a fantastic person, in love with life and our world. He ate in all the best restaurants and I often cooked for him. After the nth compliment, he asked me if I wanted to work at his restaurant, the Sangallo, on Sundays, which was my day off. He gave me carte blanche for 25 meals. I drew up the menu and he did the shopping. Gianfranco who showed me Rome, Gianfranco who treated me like his son. And we also organized unforgettable weekends in Umbria at the farmhouse of his good friend, Andrea. I cooked with Federico who is from San Giustino. Then Hervé arrived with his friend Francisco who also worked for Gagnaire

Antonio in his family house
in Depressa

and is now the catering boss at Potel et Chabot. And many French cook friends. Each one brought exceptional things—rare champagnes and vintage wines, superlative Italian and French reds and a lot of Burgundy. Among our friends was the owner of a wine cellar who subsidized this happy epicurean band. We spent memorable days and Federico's father, an experienced truffle hunter, also contributed. We repeated this experience many times, even when my Rome period was over.

They were good years. I cooked and had fun. The atmosphere was magical and Luciana and I were together. The customers were happy. Until, one day, at the Sangallo, a woman told me she had eaten so well that she wanted to tell the director of a very exclusive hotel in Porto Ercole. She called her immediately and things developed fast. I had never heard of the Pellicano and I was thunderstruck. It was a fantastic, well-managed place and Cinzia Fanciulli, the general manager, quickly set up an interview. I accepted immediately. It was an exceptional opportunity in a place of rare beauty.

Later, she told me that she had been struck by how simply I had admitted everything I didn't know how to do. Normally, young chefs were arrogant. She explained the importance of breakfasts, banquets and room service. For me, it was all new. My first time as executive chef. The 2002 season. Since my school days, Michelin had already been one of my myths. In 2004, Nicola Di Lena arrived and I saw that the kitchen was evolving. Things were changing. I had a team that wanted to grow. And in 2007 we received our first star. I was with Gianni Alocci, my food and beverage manager, in the Basque Country, and he said: 'We have to go to Milan. You've received a star.' Gianni and I have done so much together. He taught me a lot. Not only a top-notch professional and wine expert, he was very good at perceiving group dynamics and he helped me develop the team, which was decisive for the results we achieved. We had been awarded one star, but I was already thinking about the second. As Dr. Sciò, owner of the Pellicano said, in life, you have to be happily unsatisfied. And he was right. The good thing about that hotel was that it was seasonal, so, every year we started from scratch. But in the winter hiatus, you could travel the world. I went to Tokyo, to the Grand Hyatt in

Roppongi, right in front of Joël Robuchon's Atelier. It was my first time in Asia and I wanted to experience everything. I was always in the kitchen, tasting a lot. Then, one day in 2010, I got a call from Milan and they told me I had been awarded a second star.
Between the two, I had done something important. I married Luciana. It was 2009. We had been living in Orbetello for a while and she was working as a housekeeper nearby. I was boning fish with Federico and I said, out of the blue: 'You know, I think I'll get married.' He thought I was joking, but I picked up the phone and called my girlfriend. No, wait. First I called the mayor who was a good friend and I explained that I wanted to surprise Luciana. I asked the mayor if we could arrange everything in three or four days. Why waste time?
So, I called Luciana, and asked her if she wanted to marry me. She was working and immediately hung up. I called her back and said, 'I spoke with the mayor', and immediately said her name. Luciana, who knows I never remember a name, even if my life depends on it, stopped to listen, because she realized I was serious.
Three days later, with relatives arriving from Apulia and Ciociaria (my wife's home), we said our 'I do's'. In a matter of minutes, we had found what to wear, the restaurant, rings and favors. Our families were furious about the lack of warning and because they wanted a big wedding in town with a hundred people. Instead, there were fourteen of us in a restaurant in Santo Stefano. I was happy. Witnesses: Tommaso, an old friend from Depressa and Rosanna, practically a sister, and two friends of the bride.
On January 31, 2013, Viola was born. Little Viola, my pride and joy."

Milan, a new beginning "I had never been to Milan, it wasn't on the list. They called me because a new luxury 5-star hotel was opening downtown. At first, I didn't want to move. I was so happy in Orbetello. After three no's, I finally said yes. I didn't know the city. It was a tremendous challenge. The project became more and more interesting and intriguing. The fact of working year-round attracted me instead of seasonally, where you had to start virtually from zero each time. All of us—me, Federico and Nicola—being able to move together was a real opportunity. And it was the right choice. Milan has given me everything. It is a city I love and which has welcomed me, and where I have the opportunity to express myself. At Seta I have carte blanche and my goal is to get a little better every day, thanks to the help of my competent and willing team. I came to the Mandarin Oriental with Federico and Nicola and without them, I would never have made the move. It is our joint project, not just mine. All the goals I have achieved in recent years is thanks to this partnership, to our great and important friendship, but one in which we are also able to joke and have fun. We are a sort of extended family." Today, in Antonio's kitchen, there are lamb, chicken, oysters and his mother's sagne—the ingredients from his story as a boy in Apulia and, later, his time in Paris, but also Rome, Zurich and Porto Ercole. His cuisine is like a memoir in which flavors are constantly being renewed. Like the notes of a scale, always recombined into new harmonies. Every day new combinations are born and many flavors are changed in the course of things, depending on the whim of the moment (right, Monsieur Gagnaire?). And watching the chef taste a dish is a ritual in itself. Fork in the left hand (of course, left-handed!), a quick poke, a tiny morsel, another quick pass over the food, and a final little taste. A moment of reflection and then a real taste. "Each dish on the tasting menu becomes a menu portion. For me, it is important to verify that what is delicious in a small amount, doesn't become boring even for a menu version." Today, Antonio is in Milan. When he returns to his native town, everyone eyes him, discreetly, with admiration, the way you do for someone who has made it. But the wonderful thing is that Antonio Guida is essentially the same person he has always been, the boy who lit the oven for the bread, determined and sincere. And who lives following his heart.

Backstage This photo was taken on August 15th in Depressa, in Michelina and Donato's home, where Antonio grew up. It was a hot morning and we had planned to photograph some of his mother's dishes. But then, given the surroundings, we decided to set the table and all sit down to eat. Antonio's mother only hesitated for an instant ('these crazy people from Milan'), and after having moved the tables and chairs and having seen to the finishing touches in the kitchen, we sat down. Little by little, relatives arrived—cousins, brothers and nieces and nephews. Menu: sagne in tomato sauce (sensational), homemade bread baked in the famous oven, melon from the garden, salad...

Oysters

“
As a boy, I ate piles of them with my cousin Filippo, but they were
Mediterranean wild oysters. Moments that were all ours, in contact
with flavors that will be etched in my memory forever.
Then I tasted my first no. 5 in Pierre Gagnaire's kitchen in Paris.
That was also a moment of no return. That moment had a before
and after and the oysters of Brittany are always present
on my menu as an antipasto or risotto.
Food is nice when it allows you to remember the important things.
”

Oysters with potatoes

friggitelli and champagne sauce

Preparation

Open the oysters in a steam oven at 90°C for a minute.
Fry the friggitelli in hot oil, strain, cool them covered, and then skin and cut into strips.

Sour cream
Sauté the shallots in the butter and thyme, add the vinegar and Champagne and reduce by half. Add the rest of the ingredients, cook for 2-3 minutes and strain.

Ravigote sauce
Whisk the egg yolks in a bain-marie with the oyster sauce, vinegar, mustard and lime juice, then drizzle in the oils while continuing to whisk. Transfer to the siphon and add 3 gas cartridges.

Purple chips
Boil the purple potatoes whole with their skins, peel and freeze them whole, then grate them onto a Silpat mat, salt and dry them at 100°C for an hour.

Ingredients for 4 servings

50 oysters
300 g "friggitelli" (sweet Italian peppers)
200 g boiled Ratte potatoes

Sour cream
370 g Seta Champagne
11C g white wine vinegar
60 g shallots
40 g algae butter
100 g Normandy butter
130 g heavy cream
50 g milk
thyme

Ravigote sauce
160 g egg yolks
2 g lime juice
40 g oyster sauce
40 g cider vinegar
7 g mustard
150 g extra virgin olive oil
150 g sunflower seed oil

Purple chips
boiled purple potatoes

To serve

Toss the boiled potatoes in butter, combine them with the ravigote sauce and pour the resulting cream onto the plate. Arrange the oysters in the center and garnish with the sour cream, friggitelli and purple potato chips.

Snails

with herb sauce, burrata cheese and zucchini blossoms

Ingredients for 4 servings

Snails
600 g snails
bay leaf
lemons
peppercorns
white wine
vinegar
salt

Snail glaze
garlic confit
white wine
thyme, marjoram, parsley
chicken stock
chicken juices

Herb sauce
100 g spinach
50 g beet greens
water, as required
olive oil, as required
salt

Tempura
250 g all-purpose flour
100 g starch
10 g salt
50 g gently whisked eggs
400 g sparkling water
2 soda cartridges

Garnish
chopped burrata cheese
zucchini blossoms
snails
tomato powder
elderberry flowers/baby greens

Preparation

Snails
Rinse the snails under running water, then place them in boiling water together with all the other ingredients. Cook for about 1-1/2 hours.

Snail glaze
Immediately before serving, toss the snails in a frying pan with oil and the garlic confit, then douse with white wine, add the chopped herbs, and glaze with stock and chicken juices.

Herb sauce
Blanch the herbs separately and blend with water, adding olive oil and salt to taste.

Tempura
Combine all ingredients, blend and fill the siphon using two soda cartridges. Before deep frying the blossoms and snails at 180°C, lightly flour them in the cornstarch and then the tempura batter.

Presentation

Place some herb sauce on the plate, add the chopped burrata cheese seasoned with oil, salt and pepper, then top with the glazed snails and garnish with elderberry flowers or baby greens.
Separately, make a sandwich with a zucchini blossom, burrata cheese and fried snails, sprinkled with tomato powder.

Sea snails

"They have the intense flavor of the sea and pair well with other fish, like sea bass, one of our classics. My mother made me a light soup with tomato and I remember her working for hours, removing them from the shell, one-by-one. To prepare them, you need a basic ingredient: patience."

Cauliflower

Ingredients for 4 servings

75 g cauliflower
100 g milk
10g heavy cream

Almond cream sauce for cauliflower
220 g slivered almonds
1 l water
50 g cauliflower cooked in milk until soft

Seafood
30 g mussels
50 g clams
30 g shrimp
unsalted butter
yuzu juice

Garnish
20 g slivered almonds
10 g julienned nori algae
edible flowers

Preparation

Bring the milk and cream to a boil, skim and boil the cauliflower for 5-6 minutes. Once cooled, fry.

Almond cream sauce for cauliflower
Bring the mixture to 95°C in Thermomix, blend well and then filter.

Seafood
Open the seafood individually, then shell and heat in the butter with water and yuzu juice.

Presentation

Pour the almond cream sauce into the center of the plate, lay the fried cauliflower on top, sprinkle with the seafood, add a bit of yuzu juice and garnish with slivered almonds toasted in the oven and toasted nori algae, julienned using scissors. Finish with edible flowers.

Sweetbreads

with bagna cauda, kidney and caviar

Preparation

Bagna cauda

After de-germing the garlic, boil it six times in water and milk, boiling until soft the sixth time.
Then blend until smooth.
Sauté the cleaned and desalted anchovies in a frying pan with a bit of oil, then combine all ingredients and blend.

Mousse

Combine all ingredients and cook in a steam oven at 85°C for approx. 15 minutes. Blend and place in a siphon.

Dandelion cream sauce

Sauté the chopped garlic until soft in a saucepan with some oil, peperoncino and anchovies. After removing the stalks, boil the dandelion leaves separately in salted water. Combine all ingredients and cook with a bit of chicken stock; blend. Add a knob of butter.

Kidney

Cook the whole kidney immersed in sunflower seed oil at 70°C until the interior registers 58°C, then continue, turning occasionally.

Ingredients for 4 servings

600 g sweetbreads
sunflower seed oil
unsalted butter
thyme
garlic
mignonette pepper

Bagna cauda base
100 g reduced cream (reduced from 200 g)
80 g anchovies (8 fillets)
25 g garlic cream sauce

Mousse
280 g egg yolks
250 g milk
120 g heavy cream
150 g bagna cauda base
20 g garlic cream sauce
5 g salt

Dandelion cream sauce
700 g dandelions
230 g spinach
60 g anchovies
2 garlic cloves
chicken stock
Normandy butter
salt
peperoncino

Kidney
kidney
sunflower seed oil
salt

Garnish
caviar
portulaca
chicken juices

Presentation

Brown the sweetbreads in sunflower seed oil, then finish with butter, thyme, garlic and mignonette pepper. Place the dandelion cream sauce on the plate, position a sweetbread in the middle, add some mousse on top and garnish with a kidney slice dredged in the cooking butter, the caviar and portulaca leaves.

Shrimps with soft-shell

crab stock and tamarillo

Preparation

Soft-shell crab stock
Blend the soft-shell crabs with all ingredients. Bring to 85°C and allow to cool off the heat for 10 minutes, then filter through etamine. Adjust salt and acidity to taste.

Tamarillo sauce
Peel the tamarillo, separate the yellow part of the fruit and steam cook with a bit of sugar syrup at 85°C for 20 minutes. Put through a chinois to drain off the liquid, then blend the solids until smooth.

Ingredients for 4 servings

600 g shrimps

Soft-shell crab stock
1 kg of soft-shell crabs
3 l water
150 g fresh ginger
100 g galanga
5 lemongrass stalks
150 g rice vinegar

Tamarillo sauce
2 tamarillos
sugar syrup

Garnish
violets

Presentation

Peel the shrimps, toss them lightly in a skillet and cut into three parts. Pour the soft-shell crab stock into the middle of a plate, place the shrimp over it and garnish with dabs of tamarillo sauce and the violets.

Partridge truffle tart

with winter vegetables, celeriac, baby greens and Périgourdine sauce

Preparation

Tart

For the filling, mince the partridge and pigeon meat using a knife; mince the lard in a meat grinder, add the cubed foie gras followed by all other ingredients and combine well.
Roll the shortcrust out in the pasta machine to a thickness of 0.5 cm and line the small ring molds, allowing the pasta to extend over the edges, allowing the pasta to extend over the edges. Fill with the meat mixture and add a whole piece of duck breast and a small piece of escaloped foie gras pre-cooked in a mixture of Vermentino wine and hydromel. Cover with a disk of puff pastry rolled to 0.4 cm thick in the pasta machine and seal the two sheets of pasta at the base using beaten egg yolk. Brush the entire tart with a mixture of egg yolk and whole egg, cut a pattern into the top and bake in a 260°C oven for 12 minutes, and let rest for 2 minutes.

Périgourdine sauce

Lightly sauté the chopped truffle in butter, add half of the reductions and the chicken juices. Taste and complete with the vinegars.

Ingredients for 4 servings

Tart

Filling

250 g partridge
250 g pigeon breast
400 g foie gras
300 g fresh lard
30 g armagnac
15 g red port
1 g pain d'epices spices
8 g salt
40 g chopped black truffle

Shortcrust

500 g all-purpose flour
175 g unsalted butter
6 g Parmesan cheese
7,5 g malt
87,5 g water
11 g salt
1 whole egg
15 g egg yolks

Puff pastry

500 g all-purpose flour
100 g Corman butter sheet
250 g water
30 g salt

duck breast
escaloped foie gras
Vermentino wine
hydromel

Périgourdine sauce

500 g chicken juices
100 g Normandy butter
100 g cubed black truffle
125 g sherry vinegar reduced to 62.5 g
125 g raspberry vinegar reduced to 62.5 g

Garnish

sauce of celeriac cooked in milk
red and white beets glazed in stock and butter
wood-ear fungus
baby greens
black truffle slices
sliced raw mushrooms

Presentation

Position the halved tart in the center of the plate. Pour a spoon of perigordine sauce next to it, then arrange the ingredients of the garnish as in the photo.

Partridge, scallions and raspberries

Ingredients for 4 servings

Scallion sauce
500 g scallions
100 g truffle water
300 g chicken stock
20 g sherry vinegar
1 garlic clove
thyme

Chartreuse sauce
90 g cubed foie gras
450 g wild duck stuffing
30 g scorzonera sauce
scorzonera trimmings and equal weight of heavy cream
30 g Jerusalem artichoke cubes
30 g parsnip cubes
30 g pan juices
salted heavy cream

Glazed scallions
scallions
chicken stock
Normandy butter
extra virgin olive oil

Partridge thighs
4 partridge thighs
scallion sauce
chicken stock
salt, pepper

Garnish
freeze-dried raspberries
Chinese cabbage
Lacinato kale powder

Preparation

Scallion sauce
Cook the scallions until very soft with the garlic and chicken stock. At the end, add the truffle water and vinegar.

Chartreuse sauce
Cook the scorzonera in the cream until very soft, then blend and salt. Parboil the parsnip cubes for 3 minutes in the salted cream, then combine all the ingredients.

Glazed scallions
Peel the scallions, leaving the tops; sauté them in oil and butter, browning well, then remove them from the heat and place on baking sheets, dividing by size. Remove the butter from the pan and deglaze with the chicken stock. Reduce to 1 l and whisk with fresh Normandy butter. Cover the scallions with the glaze and bake in a 180°C oven, 15 minutes for the small scallions, 25 minutes for the large. Sieve the glaze through a chinois and set aside for plating.

Partridge thighs
Sear the thighs in a pan and cover with the scallion sauce diluted with chicken stock. Add salt and pepper. Bring the centers of the thighs to a temperature of 45°C, cool, debone and cut into cubes.

Presentation

Pour the scallion sauce onto the plate, add the cubes of partridge meat and the Chartreuse sauce, and garnish with Lacinato kale powder, freeze-dried raspberries and a dried Chinese cabbage leaf.

Sweetbreads

with giblets and carrot purée

Preparation

Sweetbreads

Place the sweetbreads in a saucepan in cold milk and boil for 2-3 minutes. Cool using ice water and then rinse and sauté in frothing butter and cinnamon.

Carrot purée

Peel and boil the carrots until very soft. Let dry in the chinois, then purée in the Thermomix with the Normandy butter and the grapefruit powder until smooth.

Grapefruit powder

Blanch the grapefruit peel in water three times, boil in the water and sugar syrup, dry at low temperature and grind to a powder.

Giblets

Sauté all the giblets in butter. Pour in the white port and reduce, and add the chopped thyme and marjoram. Add the chicken juices and stock. Cook for 3-4 minutes at 90°.

Ingredients

Sweetbreads

180 g sweetbreads per serving
100 g unsalted butter
20 g cinnamon
cold milk

Carrot purée

500 g cooked carrots
250 g Normandy butter
grapefruit powder, to taste

Grapefruit powder

100 g water
100 g sugar
3 g grapefruit peel

Giblets

200 g sweetbread scraps
50 g chicken livers
50 g rabbit kidneys
50 g rabbit heart
70 g cockscombs
70 g chicken stomach
chicken juices
chicken stock
Port wine
unsalted butter
thyme and marjoram

Garnish

mixed baby greens
flowers
baby carrots

Presentation

Create a circle with the carrot purée, place the giblets in the center and arrange over them the sweetbreads skewered on cinnamon sticks. Then drizzle with the carrot purée, sprinkle over the grapefruit powder and garnish with the mixed greens, flowers and baby carrots.

Cuttlefish ink risotto

with needle squid and turmeric sauce

Ingredients for 4 servings

Risotto
90 g Carnaroli rice
0.2 dl white wine
1 bay leaf
1 garlic clove
5 dl vegetable stock
extra virgin olive oil
bisque
cuttlefish ink
sour butter
Normandy butter
Espelette pepper
grated Parmesan cheese
fresh sage

Turmeric sauce
500 g Arborio rice
1/2 l chicken stock
2 spoonfuls turmeric powder
1 spoonful Madras curry powder
50 g Normandy butter
50 g grated Parmesan cheese
1 garlic clove, unpeeled
1 bay leaf
extra virgin olive oil, as required
salt

Dried sage
sage leaves
oil

Garnish
dried sage
needle squid
peas

Preparation

Risotto

In a pre-heated rondeau pan, add a bit of oil, the bay leaf and unpeeled garlic clove, then toast the rice. Salt immediately and add and boil off the white wine. Add the hot vegetable stock, non-reduced bisque and cuttlefish ink, then finish cooking the rice.
Stir in the sour butter, Normandy butter, Espelette pepper, Parmesan cheese, fresh sage and extra virgin olive oil.

Turmeric sauce

In a pre-heated rondeau pan, add a bit of oil, the bay leaf and unpeeled garlic clove, then toast the rice and salt immediately.
After having added the chicken stock, add the turmeric and curry and continue cooking on low heat until the rice is very soft.
Alternate the stock and water so that the flavor of the sauce does not become too strong.
When cooked, stir in the butter and Parmesan cheese, then process in a food processor, adjusting the density and flavor.

Dried sage

Cover a plate with plastic wrap and brush with oil. Arrange the sage leaves over it and cover with another sheet of plastic wrap. Make small holes around the leaves and microwave for about 3 minutes until the leaves are dry and crunchy.

Presentation

Use a mold to plate the rice and surround with turmeric sauce.
On top, arrange the needle squid and blanched peas, and garnish with a dried sage leaf. Serve.

Seafood sagne

with shellfish tripe sauce

Preparation

Sagne
Mix all ingredients, roll out the pasta and cut into narrow tagliatelle, then roll them up to create the sagne.

Shellfish stock
Sauté the vegetables with the lemongrass and ginger. Separately, lightly brown the lobster heads, then add the white wine and cognac and boil off. Add the vegetables followed by the bisque, fumet and stock. Simmer for about 1-1/2 hours over low heat. Strain.

Tripe sauce
Sauté a brunoise of one carrot, one stalk of celery and one onion, together with two bay leaves. Add the tripe and boil off the cooking liquid. Add the bisque and boil until done, then blend the mixture.

Sagne sauce
In a frying pan, place the garlic confit, shallot confit and mashed puntarelle cooked in the bisque. Cook over low heat until soft, then add part of the shellfish stock and half a spoonful of the tripe sauce. Toss the cooked pasta in the pan, then add the shelled seafood, baby spinach and peperoncino. Drizzle the pasta with extra virgin olive oil and the emulsified fumet.

Presentation

Create a layer of the tripe sauce on the bottom of the plate, place over it the sagne and garnish with the raw puntarelle in carpaccio style.

Ingredients for 4 servings

Sagne pasta
300 g all-purpose flour
200 g semolina flour
100 g rye flour
180 g water
1 whole egg or 60 g pasteurized egg
40 g extra virgin olive oil

Shellfish stock
6 lobster heads
2 lemongrass stalks
20 g fresh ginger
celery, carrot, onion (1 piece)
white wine
cognac
2 l bisque
2 l fumet
2 l chicken stock

Tripe sauce
500 g boiled tripe
bisque
celery, carrot, onion, bay leaf

Sagne sauce
garlic
shallots
peperoncino
shrimps
mussels
clams
baby spinach
puntarelle
bisque

Garnish
raw puntarelle

Soft-shell crabs

"I love them. These come from the Orbetello lagoon and I use them to reinforce a broth or a sauce. In Tuscany they are called 'femminelle'."

Farfalle pasta

with seafood, hermit crab sauce and coconut

Preparation

Farfalle pasta

Mix all ingredients, then create farfalle pasta.

Spider crab base

In a sauce pan with salted water, add Sarawak peppercorns and the bay leaf. Add the spider crabs, head-down in the water, and cook for about 4 minutes. Remove the crabs from the water and place them head-down in a Gastronorm for 10 minutes.
Remove the crab meat from the shell and put aside; place the crab cooking water in a Hotmix and bring to 55°C, then filter.

Hermit crab sauce

Bring the bisque to a boil, add the spider crab base, ginger, coriander, lime juice, salt and pepper. Blend, sieve in a chinois and add the coral roe.
Be careful not to let the sauce boil.

Ingredients for 4 servings

Farfalle pasta
150 g all-purpose flour
75 g semolina
185 g egg yolks

Spider crab base
2 Sarawak peppercorns
1 bay leaf
2 spider crabs

Hermit crab sauce
150 g spider crab base
250 g bisque
4 g fresh ginger
10 g coral roe
2 leaves of fresh coriander
lime juice
salt, pepper

Pan juices
Normandy butter
lime zest
julienned mint
crayfish
razor clams
mussels
lupins

Garnish
coconut flour
parsley sauce
spider crab meat

Presentation

Boil the farfalle pasta for a few minutes in salted water, then toss with the pan juices. Arrange the pasta in the center of the plate, garnish with coconut flour, parsley sauce and hermit crab meat and, to finish, at the table, pour the hermit crab sauce directly into the plate to create a soup.

Spaghetti with mackerel sauce and squids

Ingredients for 4 servings

300 g spaghetti

Mackerel marinade
1 l white wine
100 g white wine vinegar
5 g parsley
5 g peppercorns
5 g bay leaves

Mackerel sauce
500 g mackerel
150 g bisque
150 g fish fumet
250 g marinade
white wine vinegar
salt

Mixed herbs
100 g parsley sauce
90 g spinach sauce
55 g beet greens sauce
40 g lemon balm sauce

Sweet red pepper mixture
100 g julienned sweet red pepper
7 g capers, desalted and chopped
4 g Taggiasca olives, chopped

Garlic sauce
fresh garlic
water and milk

Basic sauce for spaghetti
shallot confit
sweet red pepper mixture
1 ladle bisque
1 ladle fumet
1 spoonful garlic sauce
fumet, emulsified
mixed herbs

Garnish
finely julienned squids
saffron pistils

Preparation

Mackerel marinade
Place all ingredients except the vinegar in a saucepan and bring to the boil, then add the vinegar and cover with plastic wrap. Allow to sit for about 15-20 minutes, then strain.

Mackerel sauce
Lay the fresh mackerel in a small Gastronorm and season with salt and a drop of vinegar. Pour over the stocks and marinade after having brought them to the boil. Cover with plastic wrap and allow to sit for 15 minutes. Blend and strain through a chinois.

Mixed herbs
Blanch the herbs separately and blend with iced water. Combine the purées and mix well.

Sweet red pepper mixture
Roast the peppers in aluminum foil in a 180°C oven for about 35-40 minutes.
Peel, remove the seeds and julienne. Then add the chopped capers and Taggiasca olives.

Garlic sauce
Clean the garlic and blanch 7 times in a mixture of half-water, half-milk. Drain and blend with a small amount of fresh milk.

Presentation

Pour the mackerel sauce on the plate. Arrange over it the spaghetti tossed with the basic sauce, garnish with the almost-raw julienned squid reheated just before serving, and two saffron pistils.

Mussels

"Versatile, perfect for sauces.
I like their savoriness and they give a dish character. I add them to hake and with delicate meats I add a mussel sauce which lends character that isn't overpowering, even though the secret is balance."

Fusilloro pasta

with mussels and cuttlefish

Ingredients for 4 servings

300 g Verrigni Fusilloro

Mussel sauce
300 g mussel scraps
70 g lobster coral roe
100 g mussel liquid

Oyster sauce
oyster scraps

Cuttlefish ink sauce
70 g shallot confit
150 g carrots
400 g fennel
150 g onion
150 g celery
16 g fennel fronds
2 kg cuttlefish heads
150 g cuttlefish ink
2 l bisque
1 l fumet

Leek and oyster sauce
400 g stewed leeks
160 g oyster scraps

Parsley coulis
parsley
water

Squid strips
3 squid
extra virgin olive oil, salt, pepper

Fusilli base
shallot confit
300 g "friggitelli", sweet Italian peppers
fumet
leek sauce
fumet, reduced and emulsified
pacotized oysters
mussel sauce
oyster sauce

Garnish
hairy mussels
needle squid
squid strips

Preparation

Mussel sauce
Blend all ingredients, filter, sous vide and pasteurize at 55°C for 6 minutes.

Oyster sauce
Blend the oyster scraps with a bit of oyster liquid.

Cuttlefish ink sauce
Stew the vegetables, add the cuttlefish heads, stew for 5 minutes, moisten with the bisque and fumet and cook slowly for about 1 hour. Add the cuttlefish ink, blend and sieve in a chinois.

Leek and oyster sauce
Stew the julienned leeks in oil and water; blend with the oyster scraps and then sieve through a chinois.

Parsley coulis
Blanch the parsley leaves for 2-3 minutes in salted water. Cool and blend with ice.

Squid strips
Clean and dry the squid, then season with oil, salt and pepper. Seal them flat in vacuum bags and cook for 1-1/2 hours at 55°C. Cool the bags in iced water. Remove the squid from the bags, dry and overlap them (at least 4 layers), then freeze and slice into thin, 1/8 in. strips using a slicer. Before serving, steam for 10 seconds.

Fusilli base
Fry the friggitelli in hot oil, strain, cool them covered, and then skin and julienne them.
Place them in a frying pan with the shallots, cover with 3 ladles of fumet and 1 spoonful of the leek and oyster sauce, and reduce by half.
Cook the Verrigni Fusilloro for 9-1/2 minutes, then add to the frying pan and allow them to cook for another 2 minutes.
Add the oyster sauce and emulsified fumet and cook for 30 seconds, then add the mussel sauce and leave on the heat a bit more.

Presentation

Arrange the fusilli on the plate, cover with the squid strips and garnish with the parsley coulis, cuttlefish ink sauce, hairy mussels and needle squid.

Risotto "in cagnone"

with vegetables, Castelmagno cheese and raspberry powder

Preparation

Risotto
Add a bit of oil to a pre-heated rondeau pan, allow it to heat up and then add the Carnaroli rice. Toast and add the white wine, allowing it to boil off. Continue cooking using the chicken stock. When done, remove from the heat, add the Normandy butter, sour butter, Parmesan and Castelmagno cheeses, oil, a drop of soy sauce and the julienned sage.

Herb sauce
Blanch the washed spinach and beet leaves and cool in iced water.
Blend until smooth in the Hotmixer.

Herbed rice sauce
Add a bit of oil to a pre-heated rondeau pan, allow it to heat up and then add the Carnaroli rice and toast it. Cook alternating the stock and water so that the flavor of the sauce does not become too strong.
Continue cooking on low heat until the rice is very soft, then add the herb cream.
When cooked, stir in the butter and Parmesan cheese, then process in a food processor. Adjust the density and flavor.

Ingredients for 4 servings

Risotto
300 g Carnaroli rice
chicken stock
40 g sour butter
30 g Normandy butter
julienned sage
Parmesan cheese aged 24 months
Castelmagno cheese
white wine
soy sauce
extra virgin olive oil

Herb sauce
500 g spinach
200 g beet greens

Herbed rice sauce
50 g rice
1/2 l chicken stock
40 g herb sauce
5 g Normandy butter
5 g grated Parmesan cheese
extra virgin olive oil, as required
salt

Garnish
raspberry powder

Presentation

Make a circle on the plate with the herbed rice sauce.
Fill the center with the rice and garnish with the raspberry power.

Cuttlefish ink spaghetti

with hairy mussels and miso sauce

Ingredients for 4 servings

300 g spaghetti

Spaghetti sauce
bisque
Friggitelli peppers
sage
cuttlefish ink
Espelette pepper
fish fumet, reduced

Miso sauce
100 g miso
8 hardboiled eggs
60 g lemon
20 g mustard
10 g fresh ginger
200 g unsalted butter
12 g rosemary infusion
130 g chicken stock

Garnish
hairy mussels

Preparation

Spaghetti sauce
Sauté the peppers with the sage and Espelette pepper, add the bisque, the fish fumet and the cuttlefish ink and reduce for a few minutes.

Miso sauce
Melt the butter in a frying pan and flavor with rosemary. Blend all ingredients in the Vitamix except the stock which should be added slowly at the end.

Presentation

Boil the spaghetti in salted water, add to a pan with the spaghetti sauce and toss with a drizzle of oil and reduced fumet. Twist the spaghetti on a meat fork and arrange them onto the plate over the miso sauce, then finish with the raw hairy mussels.

Ravioli stuffed with hummus

eggplant and robiola cheese

Preparation

Egg pasta

Prepare the pasta and allow to rest.

Hummus

Allow the chick peas to soak overnight, then simmer in water with celery, carrot, onion and garlic.
When cooked, salt and allow them to sit, then blend with a bit of the cooking water until smooth.
Add all the other ingredients, then add the gelatin softened in a bain-marie. Cool and add the soft-whipped cream.
Place in a pastry bag and refrigerate.

Caprino cheese sauce

Soften the goat cheese with the cream and blend, then salt and pepper to taste.

Eggplant caviar

Wash the eggplant, make 4 small gashes and insert the garlic cloves and fry at 180°C in sunflower seed oil. Dry and finish cooking in the tomato sauce and basil for 5 minutes, turning the eggplant a few times.
Cool, remove the garlic and slice thinly with a knife.
Right before serving, heat in olive oil and julienned basil.

Tomato pasta sauce

Cube the eggplant, sauté in oil, add the tomatoes, quartered, and the pasta, then cover with chicken stock. Cook for 25 minutes; in risotto style, mix in butter, Parmesan cheese, basil and tomato paste. Blend and strain through a chinois.

Ingredients for 4 servings

Egg pasta
150 g all-purpose flour
75 g semolina
185 g egg yolks

Hummus
300 g chick pea
celery, carrot, onion, garlic
7.5 g tahini
lemon juice
1 g cumin
1 g garlic confit
7 g leaf gelatin
75 g soft-whipped cream

Caprino cheese sauce
fresh caprino cheese
heavy cream
salt, pepper

Eggplant caviar
1 eggplant
4 garlic cloves
tomato sauce
basil
sunflower seed oil

Tomato pasta sauce
125 g dry short pasta
200 g vine tomatoes
150 g eggplant
1/2 tbsp tomato paste
unsalted butter
Parmesan cheese
fresh basil leaves
chicken stock

Garnish
tomato powder
fresh basil leaves

Presentation

Fill the ravioli with the hummus. Cook in boiling salted water and toss in a skillet with butter and basil. Place in the center of a plate the pasta sauce, caprino cheese and eggplant caviar; lay the ravioli on top, garnished with tomato powder and fresh caprino sauce. Top with basil leaves.

Risotto with anise, artichokes and truffle

Preparation

Risotto

Cook the rice for 11 minutes, adding a whole star anise for each serving. Two minutes from the end of cooking, again for each serving, add a spoonful of artichoke sauce. Stir in 1/3 of the Normandy butter, 1/3 of the sour butter, 1/3 of the truffle butter, the Castelmagno and Parmesan cheeses, oil and soya. Remove the star anise.

Artichoke sauce

Trim the artichokes and remove the choke. Sauté, without browning, with garlic, shallots and anise. Add some wine and allow it to evaporate, then add stock and water. When they have become tender, blend into a smooth cream. Strain and retain the cooking water.

Artichoke rice sauce

Cook the rice as a risotto until very soft. Blend into a smooth cream, adding the artichoke water and artichoke sauce.

Truffle butter

In a mixer, blend the butter and truffle paste.

Red wine glaze

Reduce the wine to 700 g and the fumet to 100 g. Combine the reduced wine, stock and fumet, then thicken with butter.

Lacinato kale powder

Dry the kale leaves on a 80°C grill, blend and pass through a fine strainer.

Ingredients for 4 servings

Risotto
300 g Carnaroli rice
star anise
artichoke sauce
Normandy butter
sour butter
truffle butter
Castelmagno cheese
Parmesan cheese
extra virgin olive oil
soya

Artichoke sauce
6 artichokes
10 g shallot confit
1 g garlic confit
1 piece of star anise
1 l stock
2 l water
white wine

Artichoke rice sauce
80 g rice
stock
Parmesan cheese
unsalted butter
artichoke water
artichoke sauce

Truffle butter
100 g Normandy butter
10 g white truffle paste

Red wine glaze
1 bottle red wine
100 g stock
200 g fish fumet
20 g unsalted butter

Lacinato kale powder
Lacinato kale leaves

Presentation

Serve the risotto in the center of the plate and sprinkle with the Lacinato kale powder. Surround with the artichoke rice sauce and drizzle with the red wine glaze.

Curdled milk gnocchi

with rabbit and mussels

Ingredients

Curds
2 l whole milk
30 g rennet

Gnocchi
350 g rennet
350 g Parmesan cheese
60 g egg whites
100 g all-purpose flour
30 g cornstarch
7 g salt
pepper

Vegetable blanquette
blanquette base
1/2 onion
1/2 celery stalk
1/2 fennel
6 mushrooms
40 g Pernod
butter

Rabbit thighs
4 thighs
blanquette

Dried parsley
parsley

Garnish
mussels
dried parsley
mushroom powder

Preparation

Curds
Heat the milk to 33°C, add the rennet and allow to cool in the refrigerator.

Gnocchi
Combine the milk curds with the Parmesan cheese and egg whites, then add the flour, cornstarch and salt. Sieve through a medium sieve and vacuum pack to make the mixture smoother.
Fill a pastry bag with a smooth tip and pre-cook in salted boiling water for about 3 minutes, then cool in iced water.
Cut into small gnocchi.

Vegetable blanquette
Sauté the vegetables in butter, add the sliced mushrooms, continue sautéing and pour in the Pernod and reduce.
Add the blanquette base and boil for about 30 minutes, then filter.

Rabbit thighs
Pan brown the thighs and place them in the blanquette and cook until they are 65°C at the center. Bone and cut into chunks.

Dried parsley
Place the parsley in a steam oven with a perforated Silpat mat for 1 minute and dry at 60°C for about an hour.

Presentation

Create a base with the blanquette, then tastefully arrange the gnocchi and decorate the plate with the mussels, rabbit thigh meat, dried parsley and mushroom powder.

Beets

"My mother also grew them at home. I like them. Now we serve them at the restaurant, crispy with bay leaf powder and orange peel."

Spaghetti with beet sauce
and shellfish carpaccio with lime

Preparation

Spaghetti
Boil the spaghetti in salted water for about 8 minutes, then toss in a frying pan with the shallot confit, garlic confit and the fried friggitelli that have been peeled and julienned. Add the slightly-reduced bisque, lime zest, grated ginger, chopped fresh dill, emulsified fumet and a lobster claw cut into cubes.

Ginger confit
Thinly slice the ginger and set under cold running water for at least an hour.
Blanch twice, starting from cold water, drain and add to the syrup prepared in advance using the water, sugar, salt and rice vinegar combined and brought to the boil.
Cover the mixture with plastic wrap and allow to cool for about a half-hour; vacuum pack and refrigerate.
The mixture must sit for at least 24 hours to allow the ginger to marinate.

Beet sauce
In a rondeau pan, place the garlic, olive oil, onion and lemongrass chopped finely. Fry gently and then add the cooked beets, cut into cubes. Add some chicken stock a simmer over low heat for about 40 minutes. Add the ginger confit and juiced beets. Allow to cook for about 20 minutes, then add the rice vinegar and cook over high heat for an additional 10 minutes. Blend the mixure in the Hotmix.

Ingredients for 4 servings

Spaghetti
300 g spaghetti
lobsters for tossing
lime zest
grated ginger
fried friggitelli
bisque
dill
fumet, emulsified
shallot confit
garlic confit

Ginger confit
1 kg sliced ginger
400 g rice vinegar
150 g water
300 g sugar
20 g salt

Beet sauce
750 g cooked beets
500 g juiced beets
20 g garlic
100 g onion
5 lemongrass stalks
300 g ginger confit
2 dl rice vinegar
1 l chicken stock
1 dl olive oil

Garnish
partially-cooked lobster
chopped and dressed with:
lime zest
grated ginger
salt, extra virgin olive oil

Presentation

Pour the beet sauce onto the plate and arrange over it the tossed spaghetti, shaped by twisting on a meat fork. Garnish with the lobster tartare.

Filled ravioli

with passatelli, foie gras and pigeon consommé

Ingredients for 4 servings

Egg pasta
150 g all-purpose flour
75 g semolina
185 g egg yolks

Filling
3 whole eggs
150 g Parmesan cheese
40 g all-purpose flour
40 g white sandwich bread crumbs
nutmeg
zest of 1/2 lemon
1.2 l chicken stock
salt, pepper

Consommé
4 chicken carcasses
4 pigeon carcasses
1 onion
2 carrots
100 g fresh ginger
chicken stock
egg whites

Garnish
cubes of sautéed foie gras
black truffle

Preparation

Egg pasta

Mound the flour and semolina in the middle of the work surface, then work in the egg yolks and roll out the dough for the ravioli.

Filling

Make the passatelli dough, combining all ingredients except the broth. Extrude the dough through a potato masher, directly into the chicken stock. Simmer gently for about 15 minutes, salt and pepper to taste. Blend and strain through a chinois. Cool and place in a pastry bag, then fill the ravioli and close them.

Consommé

Clean all the carcasses well, then place them in the chicken stock together with the onion, carrots and ginger and simmer for about 3 hours. Strain and allow to cool.
Once the broth has cooled, add the chicken and egg whites blended in a food processor. Stir well and cook on low heat, covered with perforated baking paper until the broth clarifies.
Remove from the heat and let sit for 10 minutes to allow all impurities to settle to the bottom of the pan, then strain.

Presentation

Boil the ravioli in salted water. Arrange them on the plate and garnish with the pan-tossed foie gras cubes and shaved black truffle. Pour over the consommé and serve.

Sorrel and oyster risotto

Preparation

Risotto
Toast the Carnaroli rice in a small amount of oil and salt, add the white wine and allow it to evaporate, then add the chicken stock and water and allow to cook for 11 minutes.
Add the Parmesan and Maccagno cheeses, Normandy butter, sour butter, extra virgin olive oil, soya, 1 spoonful of oyster sauce, chives, tarragon and black pepper.

Siphoned sorrel
In the Vitamix, slowly blend the eggs with the oil to make mayonnaise. Add 1/2 of an ice cube, the raw sorrel and the lemon juice, adjust the salt and place in the siphon with two gas cartridges.

Cuttlefish ink sauce
Cook the rice as a risotto until very soft, add the Parmesan cheese and Normandy butter, mix until smooth and add the cuttlefish ink.

Oyster sauce
Blend the oyster scraps until smooth and strain through a chinois.

Ingredients for 4 servings

Risotto
Carnaroli rice
chicken stock
sour butter
Normandy butter
julienned sage
Parmesan cheese aged 24 months
grated Maccagno cheese
white wine
chives
tarragon
black pepper
soya
oyster sauce
extra virgin olive oil
salt

Siphoned sorrel
3 poached eggs
300 g sorrel
sunflower seed oil
lemon juice
salt

Cuttlefish ink sauce
200 g rice
chicken stock
Parmesan cheese
Normandy butter
cuttlefish ink

Oyster sauce
oyster scraps

Garnish
finely chopped chives
chopped tarragon
Ratte potatoes, cooked and mashed with a fork
mimosa egg yolk
sorrel leaves
sliced oysters
Greek lemon cubes

Presentation

Place the blended rice on the plate, cover with the siphoned sorrel and finish with the cuttlefish ink sauce and all other garnishes.

Mullets

"They are always on my menus. I use the roe, the liver
and the delicate flesh that is intense,
firm and lean at the same time."

Mullet wrapped in beet greens

with spider crab sauce and sea snails

Ingredients

600 g whole mullets
coriander
beet green leaves
salt

Beet green glaze
200 g fumet
150 g bisque
Normandy butter
beet green ribs

Snail glaze
300 g bisque
200 g fumet
100 g chicken stock
60 g algae butter
20 g Cannellini purée
sea snails

Spider crab base
4 Sarawak peppercorns
2 bay leaves
2 spider crabs

Spider crab sauce
300 g spider crab base
500 g bisque
8 g fresh ginger
20 g fresh red roe
5 coriander leaves
lime juice
salt, pepper

Preparation

Beet green glaze
Reduce the fumet and bisque and emulsify with the butter. Peel the beet green ribs and blanch in boiling water to which lemon has been added. Finish cooking in the glaze and serve.

Snail glaze
Reduce the liquids and add the cannellini purée and butter. Use to reheat and glaze the pre-boiled and shelled sea snails.

Spider crab base
Place the pepper and bay leaves in a pan of salted water. Add the spider crabs, head-down, and cook for about 4 minutes. Remove the crabs from the water and place them head-down in a Gastronorm for 10 minutes.
Remove the crab meat from the shell; place the crab cooking water in a Hotmix and bring to 55°C, then filter.

Spider crab sauce
Bring the bisque to a boil, add the spider crab base, ginger, coriander, lime juice, salt and pepper. Blend, add the red roe and sieve in a chinois.
Be careful not to let the sauce boil.

Presentation

Bone the mullet and remove the backbone. Season with salt and coriander leaves, then wrap with a beet green leaf blanched in salted water. Sauté in a frying pan and serve with the beet green ribs and sea snails, arranged over a layer of spider crab sauce on the plate.

Beet greens

"It has a delicate flavor and adds
a hint of vegetable to a dish.
The leaves are ideal for giving color and vibrancy,
ribs are more versatile."

Turbot with wine sauce

and carrot reduction sauce

Ingredients for 4 servings

500 g turbot
butter
sunflower seed oil
thyme
mignonette pepper

Port and sake glaze
20 g sugar
1 garlic clove
2 bay leaves
peppercorns
1 l merlot red wine
100 g port
200 g fumet
70 g sake
70 g chicken juices
15 g reduced sherry vinegar
80 g Normandy butter
50 g oil
16 g radishes
85 g oysters

Carrot glaze
250 g carrot juice (1 l reduced to 250 g)
90 g tomato paste
90 g reduced sherry vinegar (reduced to 1/3)
120 g chicken stock
60 g Normandy butter
90 g chicken juices
3 g Espelette pepper (pan toasted)
12 g cumin seeds (pan toasted)

Marinated chanterelle mushrooms
1 l water
400 g oil
200 g lemon juice
6 tsp black pepper
6 tsp coriander seeds
4 bay leaves
50 g raisins

Glazed baby carrots
baby carrots
carrot glaze
salt

Garnish
glazed baby carrots
late chicory tips
julienned radishes
oyster tartare
marinated chanterelle mushroom tartare
small marinated chanterelle mushroom

Preparation

Port and sake glaze
Caramelize the sugar with the garlic, bay leaves and peppercorns; add the red wine, port and fumet and reduce to 200 g; add the rest of the ingredients, heat, blend and strain.

Carrot glaze
Combine the ingredients and heat; leave to seep for 10 minutes, strain and blend.

Marinated chanterelle mushrooms
Combine all ingredients except the raisins and mushrooms; boil for 20 minutes, then pass through a chinois to create the marinade. Clean the chanterelle mushrooms and sort into large and small. Sauté them separately and place them in the marinade with the raisins for 2 hours. Drain and refrigerate the small mushrooms whole; chop the large ones into a tartare and vacuum seal.

Glazed baby carrots
Peel and shape the baby carrots; salt and vacuum pack them with double their weight of carrot glaze. Cook in a steam oven until done, then remove them when still warm and drain away the glaze. Refrigerate.

Presentation

Lightly brown the turbot in sunflower seed oil, then finish cooking in butter, mignonette pepper and thyme.
Trim the ends of the fish and brush only the top with the carrot glaze. Place the oyster tartare and marinated chanterelle mushrooms on top, mixing them and seasoning with oil and salt.
Add the chicory and julienned radishes seasoned with oil and salt, the glazed baby carrots and a small marinated mushroom.
Finally, place the whole turbot on the plate, drizzled with the port and sake glaze.

Hake with potatoes and mussels and shiso sauce

Preparation

Hake
Salt the hake and steam for 10 minutes, then drizzle with the fish cream sauce.

Fish cream sauce
Prepare a roux with the flour and butter, add the fumet and the bay leaves and cook for 10 minutes.

Base sauce
Boil the Ratte potatoes, unpeeled, for 20 minutes. Peel them and mash with a fork.
Open the mussels and remove from the shells; chop with a knife.
Place the butter in a small pan; add the potatoes, mussels and chopped herbs and salt to taste.

Shiso sauce
Place all ingredients in a small pan, bring to the boil, salt and pepper to taste, blend and sieve through a chinois. Refrigerate.

Spinach sauce
Blanch the washed spinach in boiling salted water; when cooked, cool in iced water.
Remove from the water, blend the mixture well and refrigerate.

Shiso cream
Blanch the green leaf shiso in boiling salted water; when cooked, cool in iced water. Remove from the water, blend the mixture well and refrigerate.

Presentation

Place the base sauce on the plate, top with the hake fillet with cream sauce, arrange over it three razor clam halves previously steamed open, then garnish with the dried leek leaves.

Ingredients for 4 servings

Hake
500 g hake
fish cream sauce
salt

Fish cream sauce
400 g fumet
20 g all-purpose flour
20 g unsalted butter
2 bay leaves

Base sauce
250 g Ratte potatoes
200 g mussels
15 g chives
10 g parsley
35 g Normandy butter

Shiso sauce
750 g fish fumet
80 g mussel liquid
80 g oyster water
30 g foie gras
25 g lemon juice
30 g Normandy butter
40 g spinach sauce
70 g shiso cream

Spinach sauce
200 g spinach

Shiso cream
green leaf shiso

Garnish
razor clams
dried leek leaves

Roast turbot with lentils

caviar, mimosa and miso and rosemary sauce

Preparation

Turbot
Simmer the turbot in butter until its center reads 55°C.
Add a pinch of pepper and thyme.

Miso sauce
Melt the butter in a frying pan and flavor with rosemary. Blend all ingredients in the Vitamix except the stock which should be added slowly at the end.

Lentils
Cook the lentils until soft; drain and refrigerate.
Combine the lentils with the herb sauce (100 g of herb sauce for every 200 g of lentils).

Herb sauce
Blanch the washed spinach and beet leaves and cool in iced water.
Blend until smooth in the Hotmixer.

Ingredients for 4 servings

Turbot
600 g turbot
unsalted butter
Sarawak pepper
sprig of thyme

Miso sauce
100 g miso
8 hardboiled eggs
60 g lemon
20 g mustard
10 g fresh ginger
200 g unsalted butter
12 g rosemary infusion
130 g chicken stock

Lentils
lentils
herb sauce

Mimosa
1 hardboiled egg yolk, sieved twice
1 hardboiled egg white, sieved twice

Herb sauce
500 g spinach
200 g beet greens

Garnish
mimosa
3 g traditional caviar
dill

Presentation

Stir the herb sauce into the lentils and arrange the mixture in a circle on the plate. Pour on the miso sauce, place a turbot fillet in the center and garnish with the egg mimosa, caviar and a sprig of dill.

John Dory with zucchini and artichoke sauce

squid tartare and sweet pepper sauce

Ingredients for 4 servings

600 g John Dory
extra virgin olive oil
salt

Sweet pepper sauce
150 g tomatoes
60 g tomato water
90 g sweet pepper
110 g sweet pepper water
extra virgin olive oil
salt

Artichoke sauce
carrot, celery, onion
8 artichokes
chicken stock
white wine

Zucchini sauce
5 g shallot confit
15 peeled zucchini
200 g bisque
400 g fumet

Sea anemone sauce
225 g sea anemone
150 g bisque
170 g fumet
70 g unsalted butter
lime zest and juice

Garnish
baby zucchini
zucchini blossoms
cacciaroli squids
lime zest

Preparation

Grill the John Dory, seasoned with salt and oil, then bake in a 160°C oven for 8 minutes

Sweet pepper sauce
Peel the tomatoes, cut them in half and roast in a 180°C oven for about 30 minutes. When roasted, put them through a chinois and drain off the water, then strain the pulp. Season the sweet peppers with salt and oil, wrap them in aluminum foil and bake in a 180°C oven for about 30 minutes. Then drain off the water in the chinois, peel them and blend the pulp. Combine the two sauces and salt to taste.

Artichoke sauce
Prepare a traditional sauté of carrot, celery and onion, then add the artichokes cut into pieces. Add the white wine and boil off and then add the chicken stock. Cook for about 30 minutes, blend and strain.

Zucchini sauce
Place the shallots in a saucepan, add the peeled zucchini and add the stocks. Cook for about 5 minutes, blend and strain.

Sea anemone sauce
Blend the sea anemone, season with the lime zest and juice, bring to 85°C and strain. Then add all the other ingredients.

Garnish
Arrange the washed zucchini blossoms on a baking sheet lined with buttered plastic wrap. Place another sheet of plastic wrap over the blossoms, poke holes in the plastic and blanch in a 90°C steam oven for 2 minutes. Arrange the blossoms on a Silpat mat and dry in an 85°C oven for about 1 hour. In the meantime, cook the whole baby zucchini in salted water. Once cooled, cut in half and brown lightly in a frying pan before serving. Clean the cacciaroli squids, separate the head from the body, cut the body in half and make some small incisions. Toss quickly in a frying pan and season with lime zest.

Presentation

Place a pasta mold in the center of the plate. Pour into it the combined zucchini and artichoke sauces, then place the John Dory on top and arrange around it the sweet pepper sauce. Glaze the fish with the sea anemone sauce, then garnish with the zucchini blossoms, the zucchini and cacciaroli squids.

Striped bass

with curry and banana sauce and Gorizia rose radicchio

To prepare

Steam the striped bass for 5-6 minutes.

Turmeric sauce

Sauté the shallots with the lemongrass, garlic, ginger, coriander, peppercorns and spices, then cook.
Add the chicken stock and reduce by half, then add the coconut milk and tapioca and continue cooking until the sauce thickens.
Add the banana and the lime juice, blend, salt to taste and, if necessary, add a dash of sherry vinegar.

Gorizia rose radicchio

Remove the outside leaves to have leaves that are all the same size and require the same cooking time. Vacuum seal the leaves and roses separately in the marinade and cook the roses at 85°C for about 30 minutes and the leaves for 20 minutes.

Ingredients

500 g striped bass

Tumeric sauce
4 shallots
3 lemongrass leaves
2 garlic cloves, crushed
40 g fresh ginger
1 tbsp coriander seeds
1/2 tbsp peppercorns
5 sprigs of fresh coriander
15 g Thiercelin hot curry
15 g Thiercelin tumeric
1 l chicken stock
1.2 l unsweetened coconut milk
20 g tapioca
juice of 2 limes
2 ripe bananas
salt
sherry vinegar

Gorizia rose radicchio
Gorizia rose radicchio
800 g blood orange juice
250 g sherry vinegar
20 g salt

Garnish
6 banana slices
3 half oyster leaves
lobster juices
Gorizia rose radicchio leaves

To serve

Garnish the striped bass with the banana slices, a Gorizia rose and the oyster leaves; arrange on the plate and garnish with the tumeric sauce and lobster juices.

Mullet, squid water and cockles

Ingredients for 4 servings

Squid stock
1 l water
2 kg cleaned squid
5 slices of ginger
3 bay leaves
anchovy oil

Mullet
mullet
coriander
salt
beet green leaves
unsalted butter

Garnish
40 g squid
beet green leaves
bay leaves
extra virgin olive oil
herb sauce
cockles
penny bun or champignon mushrooms
rehydrated wakame algae

Preparation

Squid stock
Blend the squid with water, place in a sauce pan with the ginger and bay leaves; bring to the boil and simmer for 30 minutes. Strain and add 15 g of anchovy oil per liter of stock.

Mullet
Bone the mullet, season with salt and fresh coriander, cut into 3 pieces and wrap one in a beet green leaf. Cook in butter with vadouvan.

Presentation

Clean the squid and brunoise cut.
Julienne the uncooked beet greens and season with a bay leaf extract made using a Green Star juicer, and bound with oil and herb sauce.
Open and shell the cockles.
Julienne the tops of the cepe or champignon mushrooms.
Pour in a plate the squid stock, then position the squid tartare and the fish cooked in a pan, finally decorate with shelled cockles, julienne of mushrooms, beet green leaves and rehydrated wakame algae.

Salt-crusted chicken served three ways

Ingredients for 4 servings

1.5 kg whole chicken
mint
marjoram
garlic
lime
salt
oil
white wine
black pepper

Salt crust
flour
egg whites
herb sauce (spinach and beet greens)
salt

Neck
chicken livers
chicken thigh
chicken fillet
pork fat
salt
pepper
cinnamon
white port

Breast
beets
new potatoes
celeriac
late Treviso red chicory
purple romanesco broccoli
cauliflower
squash
chicken juices with white Malvasia wine

Thigh
fregola pasta
chicken stock
unsalted butter
Parmesan cheese
parsley
tarragon
chicken juices

Preparation

Clean the chicken of its giblets and tie it. Marinate it with all the ingredients, brown and then cover with the salt crust, previously prepared and spread to thickness of about 1/8 in.
Roast in a 150°C oven for about 35 minutes; let rest for 10 minutes.
Remove the salt crust and cut into portions, separating the breasts and thighs, then serve in three successive courses:

Course #1 – Neck
Process all ingredients into a smooth mixture and, using a piece of plastic wrap, form the mixture into the shape of a chicken neck and simmer in water for about 30 minutes.
Slice and serve in chicken stock laced with ginger.

Course #2 – Breast
Cook all vegetables separately in salted water. Before serving, toss with oil in a frying pan and arrange geometrically on the plate. In the center, place the chicken breast topped with the chicken pan juices laced with Malvasia white wine.

Course #3 – Thighs
Debone the thighs and finish cooking (the thighs require more time than the breasts).
In the meantime, prepare the fregola pasta as risotto using the chicken stock and stir in the butter, Parmesan cheese, parsley and tarragon.
Arrange the fregola pasta on the plate, place a chicken thigh on top and spoon over the chicken pan juices.

Fillet of beef with chopped herbs

artichokes and choron sauce

Preparation

Fillet of beef

Sear the four beef fillets on all sides, cook in a knob of butter with thyme and garlic for 5 minutes per side and let rest for at least 10 minutes.
Separately, mince the fillet into a tartare and season with salt and extra virgin olive oil.

Choron sauce

Prepare a bernaise sauce, then add the tomato confit sauce. Sieve through a chinois and place in the siphon.

Artichoke sauce

Lightly sauté the diced carrot, celery and onion, add the cleaned artichokes cut in half and the white wine and boil off.
Add the chicken stock and cook until soft.
Blend part of the artichokes and slice the rest; combine to create a chunky artichoke sauce.

Ingredients for 4 servings

Fillet of beef
4 servings of 150 g whole fillet each
120 g of fillet for tartare
butter
garlic
thyme
salt
extra virgin olive oil

Choron sauce
80 g egg yolks
200 g clarified butter
20 g water
10 g reduced vinegar
100 g tomato confit sauce

Artichoke sauce
carrot
celery stalk
onion
8 artichokes
chicken stock
white wine

Garnish
dried curly cabbage leaves
raw artichokes
edible flowers
meat juices

Presentation

Place the artichoke sauce in the center of the plate; over it add a fillet and some of the tartare, then garnish with raw, julienned artichokes and a dried cabbage leaf. To the side, add a generous spoonful of choron sauce and drizzle over the meat juices.

Stuffed wild duck

with cabbage roulade and spring onion sauce

Preparation

Wild duck stuffing

Grind the thighs and fatty and lean neck meat, then cube the rest of the ingredients and combine all in a bowl.

Wild duck breasts

Clean the duck breasts and remove the skin; weigh them and cover the upper part with the stuffing which must be half of their weight. Cover with the chicken moussette and wrap with the pork caul fat. Cook in a frying pan with butter and thyme for 12 minutes, then allow to rest for at least 6 minutes.

Spring onion sauce

Julienne the spring onions, cook with the butter on low heat without allowing them to brown, then add the sage and cream and bring to a boil. Blend.

Chartreuse sauce

Cook the scorzonera in the cream until very soft, then blend and salt. Parboil the parsnip cubes for 3 minutes in the salted cream, then combine all the ingredients.

Cabbage leaves

Parboil the cabbage leaves separately. Cool them in iced water and lay them to dry on paper towels. Roll gently with a rolling pin to flatten them as much as possible, then cut into squares and fill with the wild duck stuffing. Place the scorzonera battonets in the center of the stuffing and form into cylinders sealed with plastic wrap.

Presentation

Escalope the wild duck breasts in half and arrange on the plate over the spring onion sauce, vapor-cooked Chartreuse sauce, stuffed cabbage and the brunoise vegetables sautéed in oil, salt and pepper.

Ingredients

Wild duck stuffing

600 g wild duck thigh
225 g fatty neck meat
90 g lean neck meat
180 g cubed foie gras
105 g chicken livers
75 g heart
30 g lungs
22 g cognac
22 g armagnac
30 g red port
25 g truffle
3 g garlic confit
4 g shallot confit
1 whole egg (with a bit of the albumen removed)

Wild duck breasts

4 wild duck breasts
chicken moussette
wild duck stuffing
pork caul fat
butter and thyme

Spring onion sauce

500 g white onion
100 g heavy cream
50 g unsalted butter
1 sage leaf

Chartreuse sauce

90 g cubed foie gras
450 g wild duck stuffing
30 g scorzonera sauce
scorzonera trimmings and equal weight of heavy cream
30 g Jerusalem artichoke cubes
30 g parsnip cubes
30 g pan juices
salted heavy cream
salt

Cabbage leaves

cabbage leaves
wild duck stuffing
scorzonera battonet

Garnish

squash brunoise
celeriac brunoise

Venison

with chestnut sauce, mango and apple

Preparation

Quickly sear the venison and then add a knob of butter, garlic and thyme; lower the heat and continue cooking 3 minutes per side. Let rest at least 10 minutes.

Fruit
Cube the mango and apple and sauté quickly with butter and lime zest.

Game juices
To the juices of the venison carcass, add the red wine reduced with cinnamon, bay leaf, thyme and cloves, then finish with a small piece of bitter chocolate.

Chestnut sauce
Cook the chestnuts in the chicken stock, Strega liqueur, fresh dill, salt and pepper. Boil until the chestnuts are very tender, then blend. Add the butter and adjust the thickness and seasoning.

Ingredients for 4 servings

400 g saddle of venison
butter
thyme
garlic

Fruit
100 g cubed mango
150 g cubed green apple
lime zest
Normandy butter

Game juices
juices of the venison carcass
red wine
cinnamon
bay leaf
thyme
cloves
bitter chocolate

Chestnut sauce
chestnuts cooked au naturel
Strega liqueur
fresh dill sprigs and seeds
chicken stock
Normandy butter
salt
pepper

Garnish
baby spinach leaves
sugar-coated almonds

Presentation

Place the chestnut sauce in the center of a plate, place the sliced venison over it and add the fruit and game juices. Garnish with the baby spinach slightly wilted in hot oil, and the chopped sugar-coated almonds.

Spiced duck

with creamy black polenta, dates and hazelnuts

Preparation

Duck breasts
Lightly sauté the duck breasts in oil and cook with a knob of butter and the mixed spices for 8 minutes. Let rest for 6 minutes and remove the skin.

Black polenta
Bring the water and salt to a boil, add the cornmeal and cook on low heat for an hour, then add the cuttlefish ink and blend.

Date sauce
Blend the skinned dates together with the hazelnuts and water, then sieve through a chinois to obtain a smooth sauce.

Lacinato kale leaves
Blanch the kale leaves in salted water, cool and dry in a low oven for an hour, then fry in sunflower seed oil.

Ingredients for 4 servings

Duck breasts
4 duck breasts
0.5 g cloves
0.5 g cardamom
0.5 g cinnamon
0.5 g Jamaica pepper
extra virgin oil
butter

Black polenta
125 g cornmeal
1 l water
1/2 tbsp cuttlefish ink
salt

Date sauce
4 fresh dates
25 g hazelnuts
200 g water

Lacinato kale leaves
Lacinato kale leaves
sunflower seed oil

Presentation

Pour some of the cuttlefish ink sauce and date sauce onto a plate, place the duck breast on top and garnish with the kale leaves.

Pigeon terrine

with Suprême sauce and giblets

Preparation

Cook the pigeon fillets in salted water for 20 seconds.

Terrine

For the pigeon mixture chop the ingredients and mix them. Alternate: 4 layers of mousseline and 3 of the pigeon mixture in a loaf pan lined with plastic wrap. Each layer must be 100 g.
Steam at 85°C for 35 minutes. The center should read 56-58°C.

Périgourdine sauce

Lightly sauté the chopped truffle in butter, add half of the reductions and the chicken juices. Taste and complete with the vinegars.

Giblet sauce

Cook the cockscombs and gizzards at 130°C, the cockscombs for 2 hours and the gizzards for 3 hours, confit with marjoram and thyme and garlic. Julienne. Place the sweetbreads in a frying pan with butter and oil, moisten with sherry vinegar, add the gizzards and cockscombs, then add the pan juices, salt and pepper.

Ingredients for 4 servings

600 g pigeon fillets
Suprême sauce

Terrine

Pigeon mixture
- 400 g pigeon breast fillets
- 170 g cubed foie gras
- 75 g chopped chicken livers
- 10 g cognac
- 10 g salt
- 1 g sage

320 g mousseline

Périgourdine sauce

1 kg chicken juices
200 g Normandy butter
200 g cubed black truffle
250 g sherry vinegar reduced to 125 g
250 g raspberry vinegar reduced to 125 g

Giblets sauce

chopped sweetbreads
cockscombs
gizzards
chopped marjoram and thyme
garlic
chicken juices
Périgourdine base
sherry vinegar
butter
extra virgin olive oil
salt, pepper

Garnish

sliced button and cepe mushrooms
truffle slices
mushroom powder (dried trumpet mushrooms)

Presentation

Spread on the Suprême sauce on the plate, then arrange over it the giblets, terrine, pigeon fillet, Périgourdine sauce and mushroom and truffle slices, and finally the mushroom powder.

Lamb in saté sauce

with zucchini "a scapece", caprino cheese and citron

Preparation

Lamb

Coat the lamb evenly with the chicken mousseline, then wrap with the pork caul fat. Brown and baste in the butter to desired level of doneness.

Stuffing for the roulade

Combine all ingredients in a bowl, except for the zucchini. Transfer the mixture to a pastry bag. Thinly slice the zucchini, season with salt and oil and bake in a steam oven at 100°C for 5 minutes. Trim off the green part and lay the slices side by side. Pipe the cream onto the zucchini and roll into a cylinder.

Zucchini sauce

Boil only the green part of the zucchini for 4-5 minutes in salted water, mix and add the rest of the ingredients.

Tomato confit

Cut the cherry tomatoes in half, season with all the ingredients and arrange cut side up on a Silpat mat; dry at 80°C for 4 hours.

Lemon purée

Blanch the lemons 3 times in a mixture of 1 l of water and 200 g of salt. Then candy in 1 l of water and 300 g of sugar. Cool and purée the whole lemon.

Presentation

Decorate the plates with dabs of the zucchini sauce and fresh baby greens. Place the lamb in the center and garnish with slices of lemon and lamb pan juices. Arrange the tomato confit and the roulade, then finish with dots of lemon purée.

Ingredients for 4 servings

Lamb

260 g lamb loin
80 g pork caul fat
180 g of chicken mousseline
butter

Stuffing for the roulade

40 g caprino cheese
60 g ricotta
50 g fennel
2 g fresh mint
zest of 1 lemon
3 100 g zucchini

Zucchini sauce

120 g zucchini
3 g fresh mint
10 g vinegar
10 g extra virgin olive oil
3 g salt
1 garlic clove

Tomato confit

16 cherry tomatoes
40 g extra virgin olive oil
5 g confectioners' sugar
zest of 1 orange
zest of 1 lemon
15 g fresh basil

Lemon purée

water
salt
sugar
lemon

Garnish

baby greens
slices of lemon
lamb pan juices

Heart

“
It all starts with heart.
When you put your heart and passion,
everything is easy and less arduous.
This one is lamb. A kind of meat I am especially fond of.
It’s almost always on my menu. I like its intense flavor.
And it’s surprising because when the meat is good quality,
the gamey aroma even becomes delicate.
This is from Tuscany.
And I make a sauce using the giblets,
sweetbreads and a bit of liver.
”

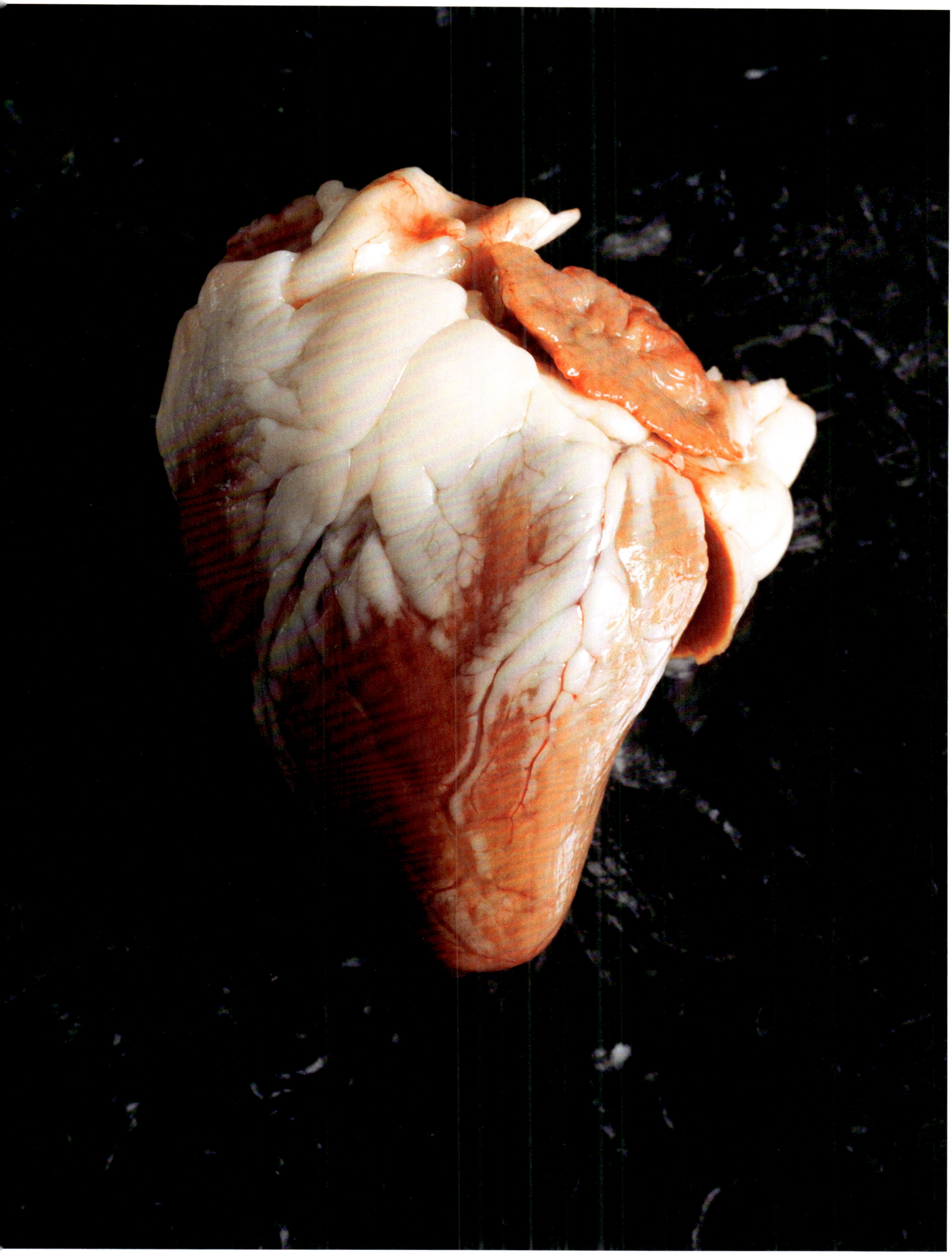

Hare Royale

Preparation

Royale stuffing

Grind the capocollo and hare.
Cube the foie gras and freeze, then hand chop the heart, lung and liver and, finally, cube the truffle.
Combine all ingredients, then add the foie gras. Salt and pepper to taste and mix in the hare blood.

Royale

Debone the hare thighs and shoulders and pound.
Partially cut the hare sirloin in half, open and pound well. Devein the foie gras and, using a piece of plastic wrap, mold by hand into a cylinder.
Marinate the shoulders, thighs and sirloin in armagnac and cognac.

Ingredients

Royale stuffing
400 g pork capocollo
500 g hare
400 g foie gras
200 g black truffle
200 g hare heart, lungs and liver
40 g parsley
10 g cognac
10 g armagnac
20 g shallot confit
100 g onion confit
10 g garlic confit
hare blood
salt
pepper

Royale
exterior:
1,250 kg hare thighs and shoulder
middle:
500 g hare sirloin
interior:
800 g foie gras

armagnac
cognac

Garnish
chocolate
Suprême sauce
wagon wheel pasta
truffle butter
chicken stock
Brussel sprouts

Presentation

Lay three sheets of plastic wrap on the work surface and salt and pepper them. Arrange the shoulders and thighs on the wrap and salt and pepper again. Arrange the first part of the stuffing in the center, place the sirloin and foie gras cylinder over it and roll and wrap with a few layers of plastic wrap.
Pierce with a fork and place the royale cylinders in red wine for 12 hours.
Drain and sous vide with the hare juices at 68°C for 24 hours.
Cool and divide into individual vacuum bags.
Heat in water, glaze with the cooking juices seasoned to taste with chocolate and Suprême sauce. Garnish with the wagon wheel pasta glazed in truffle butter, chicken stock and Suprême sauce.
Complete with Brussel sprouts tossed in oil.

Butter

“At Seta, I like to serve it two ways: one cone-shaped with algae and the other salted with Altamura bread. In the kitchen, I use it with both meat and fish.”

Mandarin orange

filled with candied kumquat and raw cacao gelato

Composition

Mandarin orange crème Chantilly
Mandarin orange and kumquat inserts
Mandarin orange glaze
Mandarin orange sauce
Raw cacao gelato
White chocolate mousse
Chestnut chocolate mousse
Almond cake

Ingredients

Mandarin orange crème Chantilly
75 g Ivoire chocolate
250 g heavy cream
grated peel of 2 mandarin oranges

Mandarin orange and kumquat inserts
100 g candied kumquat seeds
100 g mandarin orange, supremed
2 g chopped coriander

Mandarin orange glaze
140 g sugar
140 g water
90 g dextrose
120 g condensed milk
9 g leaf gelatin
50 g cocoa butter
15 g yellow cocoa butter
140 g Absolut leaf gelatin

Mandarin orange sauce
125 g mandarin orange purée
125 g fresh-squeezed mandarin orange
grated peel of 2 mandarin oranges

Raw cacao gelato
250 g milk
150 g heavy cream
80 g egg yolks
50 g sugar
25 g finely chopped cocoa beans

White chocolate mousse
225 g heavy cream
320 g Ivoire chocolate
2 g leaf gelatin
125 g custard

Preparation

Mandarin orange crème Chantilly
Boil the cream with the mandarin orange zest and pour over the chocolate. Let stand in the refrigerator overnight; the next day, whip the crème Chantilly in the Kitchenaid mixer.

Mandarin orange and kumquat inserts
Coarsely chop the kumquat and mandarin oranges, combine well and add the chopped coriander. Place the mixture in small semi sphere molds and freeze.

Mandarin orange glaze
In a saucepan, boil the condensed milk, sugar, water and dextrose. Add the leaf gelatin, pre-softened in cold water for 10 minutes. Add the Absolut gelatin and cocoa butter. Finally, cream the yellow/red cocoa butter for 3 minutes at maximum speed in a mixer.

Mandarin orange sauce
Combine all ingredients and reduce.

Raw cacao gelato
Prepare the custard, pour into the Pacojet beakers and freeze.

White chocolate mousse
Prepare a ganache with the cream and chocolate. When it reaches 40°C, add the gelatin and then the custard.

Chestnut chocolate mousse
Prepare a ganache with the cream and chocolate. When it reaches approx. 40°C, add the gelatin and then the Italian meringue and soft-whipped cream.

Almond cake
Cream the butter and sugar, add the eggs, gradually add the flours, baking powder, salt and, finally, the almond cream. Spread the mixture on a Silpat baking mat to a thickness of approx. a quarter-inch and bake in a 170°C oven for 15 minutes.

Chestnut chocolate mousse
140 g equatorial chocolate
95 g heavy cream
65 g chestnut paste
6 g leaf gelatin
65 g Italian meringue
150 g soft-whipped cream

Almond cake
225 g unsalted butter
25 g almond cream
125 g white sugar
1 g salt
250 g whole eggs
180 g all purpose flour
100 g almond flour
4 g baking powder

Presentation

Fill a small-tipped pastry bag with the chestnut chocolate mousse and create a line that divides the plate in half. With the same mousse, create three dollops and place the marron glacé pieces on top. Fill the mandarin orange with the mandarin crème Chantilly, the inserts and the almond cake; glaze and place it to one side on the plate. Complete with the supremed mandarin orange and the raw cacao gelato.

Tobacco

Composition

Licorice parfait
Tobacco
Spiced pears
Coffee sauce

Ingredients

Licorice parfait
225 g heavy cream
65 g white sugar
25 g water
80 g egg yolk
2.5 g leaf gelatin
3 g licorice powder

Tobacco
100 g organic tobacco
100 g syrup 1:1

Spiced pears
100 g pears
50 g syrup 1:1
star anise
black pepper
vanilla pods
green cardamom

Coffee sauce
75 g heavy cream
125 g fresh whole milk
40 g egg yolks
25 g sugar
25 g coffee beans
2 short "ristretto" cups of espresso coffee

Preparation

Licorice parfait
Prepare a pâte à bombe with sugar at 121°C and egg yolk; when still warm, add the pre-softened gelatin. Add the licorice powder, followed by the soft-whipped cream. Spread the mixture approx. 1/2 in. thick on a Silpat mat and freeze.

Tobacco
Soak the tobacco in water to eliminate its bitterness and repeat over a period of 3 days; store in the syrup. Spread the tobacco leaves on a Silpat mat and bake in a 200°C oven for about 10 minutes.

Spiced pears
Peel the pears, slice into wedges and place them in a vacuum bag with the syrup and spices. Cook in a steam oven for approx. 20 minutes. N.B.: the pears must be soft.

Coffee sauce
Combine all ingredients and prepare a custard.

Presentation

Pour some coffee sauce on the plate and position a spiced pear wedge in the center; create multiple layers of the tobacco and licorice parfait, and place on top of the pear.

Strawberry and tomato cheesecake

with saffron gelato

Composition

Strawberry and tomato water
Strawberry jam
Hazelnut cake
Cheesecake
Basil parfait
Saffron gelato
Sugar wafer

Strawberry and tomato water
100 g tomato water
100 g strawberry water
15 g TPT syrup
10 g St. Germain

Strawberry jam
500 g strawberries
50 g sugar

Hazelnut cake
225 g unsalted butter
25 g hazelnut cream
125 g white sugar
125 g light brown sugar
1 g salt
1/2 vanilla bean
250 g whole eggs
75 g cornstarch
75 g rice starch
100 g almond flour
4 g baking powder

Cheesecake
50 g egg whites
100 g sugar
250 g heavy cream
8 g leaf gelatin
200 g cream cheese
100 g fresh caprino cheese

Basil parfait
100 g sugar
50 g egg whites
250 g heavy cream
3 g leaf gelatin
100 g basil chlorophyll

Preparation

Strawberry and tomato water
Combine ingredients.

Strawberry jam
Combine ingredients.

Hazelnut cake
Cream the butter and sugar, add the eggs, gradually add the flours, baking powder, vanilla, salt and, finally, the hazelnut cream. Spread the mixture on a Silpat baking mat to a thickness of approx. a quarter-inch and bake in a 170°C oven for 15 minutes.

Cheesecake
Prepare an Italian meringue; when still warm, fold in the gelatin. When the mixture is cool, add the cream cheese and the caprino cheese, then the soft-whipped cream.

Basil parfait
Prepare an Italian meringue, then add the leaf gelatin and allow to cool. Add the soft-whipped cream and the basil chlorophyll.

Saffron gelato
Combine all ingredients and prepare a custard to 86°C, then pour into the Pacojet beakers and freeze.

Sugar wafer
Heat the two sugars to 150°C, remove from heat and add the tartaric acid, chocolate, vanilla and strawberry powder, then pour onto a Silpat mat and allow to cool. Pulse in a food processor to a fine crumb. Sieve onto a Silpat mat and bake at 170°C for 5 minutes to create a sugar wafer.

Saffron gelato
350 g milk
250 g heavy cream
60 g egg yolks
60 g sugar
1/2 saffron packet
4 saffron pistils

Sugar wafer
175 g fondant sugar
75 g glucose
2 drops of tartaric acid
45 g Ivoire chocolate
1 vanilla bean
10 g strawberry powder

Presentation

Create a square on the plate using the strawberry jam, pour onto the square the strawberry and tomato water, then place the cheesecake in the center. On top of the cheesecake, make three smooth dollops of basil parfait using a pastry bag and add a saffron gelato quenelle and gold leaf.

Honey and sage soufflé

with coconut blancmange and beet and citrus sorbet

Preparation

Honey and sage soufflé
Prepare a honey and sage custard. For the soufflé whip the egg whites with the sugar and gently fold in the custard. Spoon the mixture into soufflé cups and bake at 180°C for 14 minutes.

Coconut blancmange
Combine the coconut milk and sugar in a saucepan and heat to 80°C. Remove from the heat and when it has cooled to 45°C, add the leaf gelatin. Allow to cool. In the meantime, soft-whip the cream and fold it in.

Beet and citrus sorbet
Combine all ingredients in a saucepan, heat to 80°C and then remove from the heat and freeze in the Pacojets.

Composition

Honey and sage soufflé
Coconut blancmange
Beet and citrus sorbet

Ingredients
Honey and sage soufflé

Honey and sage custard
1 l whole milk
250 g honey
200 g 85% Abinao chocolate
80 g cornstarch
250 g egg yolks
sage

Soufflé
75 g egg whites
15 g white sugar
90 g honey and sage custard

Coconut blancmange
800 g coconut milk
60 g sugar
500 g heavy cream
16 g leaf gelatin

Beet and citrus sorbet
250 g juiced beet
1 lemongrass stick
35 g dextrose
35 g liquid glucose
15 g grapefruit juice
1.5 g carob flour

Presentation

Serve the soufflé in the cups, accompanied by the blancmange on a dessert plate. Garnish the blancmange with the coconut chips and beet and citrus sorbet.

Apple fondant

lychee and pomegranate sauce
and pain brioche and cognac gelato

Composition

Golden Delicious apples
Lychee and pomegranate sauce
Hazelnut cake
Quince jam
Pain brioche and cognac gelato

Golden Delicious apples
soft caramel
- 180 g light brown sugar
- 140 g liquid glucose
- 150 g heavy cream
- 150 g lychee juice
- 30 g unsalted butter
- 1 vanilla bean

3 Golden Delicious apples

Lychee and pomegranate sauce
250 g juiced pomegranate
100 g lychee purée
25 g TPT syrup

Hazelnut cake
225 g unsalted butter
25 g hazelnut cream
125 g white sugar
125 g light brown sugar
1 g salt
1/2 vanilla bean
250 g whole eggs
15c g pastry flour (or cornstarch)
100 g hazelnut flour
4 g baking powder

Quince jam
500 g quinces
15c g sugar
30 g lemon juice

Pain brioche and cognac gelato
250 g milk
15c g heavy cream
80 g egg yolks
50 g sugar
350 g pain brioche
50 g cognac

Preparation

Golden Delicious apples
Prepare some caramel, then peel and thinly slice the apples; arrange them in layers. Place them with the caramel in a vacuum bag, cook at 70°C for 5-6 hours; preserve the juice and trim the apples to create 4 in. x 1-1/2 in. rectangles.

Lychee and pomegranate sauce
Use a centrifugal juicer to prepare the pomegranate juice; add the lychee purée and TPT syrup.

Hazelnut cake
Cream the butter and sugar, add the eggs, gradually add the flours, baking powder, vanilla, salt and, finally, the hazelnut cream. Spread the mixture on a Silpat baking mat to a thickness of approx. a quarter-inch and bake in a 170°C oven for 15 minutes.

Quince jam
Combine the ingredients and cook on low heat for 20 minutes.

Pain brioche and cognac gelato
Cube the pain brioche, place on a baking sheet and toast in the oven at 200°C for 10 minutes. In the meantime, prepare a custard. Pour the custard over the toasted pain brioche and let sit for about an hour. Sieve through a chinois and add the cognac; fill the Pacojet beakers and freeze.

Presentation

Create a 5 in. circle with the quince jam in the middle of the plate; pour into the center the lychee and pomegranate sauce, then arrange in the center two rectangles of the layered Golden Delicious apples on top of the hazelnut cake. Complete with a quenelle of the pain brioche and cognac gelato placed between the two apple rectangles.

Ginger Royale

mango with passion fruit and lemongrass gelato

Composition

Ginger Royale
Mango and passion fruit mousse
Ginger chips
Mango cubes
Lemongrass gelato
Edible flowers
Passion fruit sauce

Ingredients

Ginger Royale
500 g heavy cream
180 g egg yolks
70 g sugar
25 g juiced ginger

Mango and passion fruit mousse
250 g mango purée
125 g passion fruit purée
75 g egg whites
150 g sugar
10 g leaf gelatin
250 g heavy cream

Ginger chips
50 g fresh ginger
confectioners' sugar

Almond cake
225 g unsalted butter
25 g almond cream
125 g white sugar
125 g light brown sugar
1 g salt
150 g whole eggs
75 g cornstarch
75 g rice starch
100 g almond flour
4 g baking powder

Lemongrass gelato
500 g fresh whole milk
210 g heavy cream
120 g white sugar
100 g lemongrass
18 g glucose
1 g carob flour
grated peel of 1 lime

Preparation

Ginger Royale
Combine the ingredients and pour the royale onto a plate, then cook in a steam oven at 86°C for 10-12 minutes.

Mango and passion fruit mousse
Prepare an Italian meringue, then add the purées, gelatin and soft-whipped cream.

Ginger chips
Thinly slice the ginger and dust with confectioners' sugar.

Almond cake
Cream the butter and sugar, add the eggs, gradually add the flours, baking powder, salt and, finally, the almond cream. Spread the mixture on a Silpat baking mat to a thickness of approx. a quarter-inch and bake in a 170°C oven for 15 minutes.

Lemongrass gelato
Prepare a neutral base with all ingredients except the lemongrass and lime; add the lemongrass and lime to the base to infuse overnight in the refrigerator. The next day, pour into Pacojet beakers and freeze.

Presentation

Serve the royale on a plate and add the mango and passion fruit mousse, lemongrass gelato and almond cake. Garnish with the passion fruit sauce, fresh mango, ginger chips and edible flowers.

Campari

Composition

35% white chocolate mousse
Grapefruit sauce
Cherry gelatin
Grapefruit and Campari sorbet
Campari wafers
Campari-marinated grapefruit
Fresh fennel

35% white chocolate mousse
Custard (300 g)
- 75 g heavy cream
- 75 g fresh whole milk
- 30 g egg yolks
- 15 g sugar

3 g leaf gelatin
225 g heavy cream
300 g 35% Ivoire chocolate

Grapefruit sauce
450 g grapefruit juice
100 g of sugar syrup 1:1
2 g xanthan gum

Cherry gelatin
110 g cherry purée
60 g syrup 1:1
30 g Campari
14 g leaf gelatin

Grapefruit and Campari sorbet
125 g grapefruit juice
25 g Campari
50 g water
30 g glucose
1 g carob flour

Campari wafers
15 g Campari
90 g water
90 g unsalted butter
15 g cornstarch

Campari-marinated grapefruit
grapefruit
Campari

Fresh fennel
fennel
Campari

Preparation

35% white chocolate mousse
Prepare the custard and when it is still warm, fold it into the white chocolate mousse, then allow it to cool and add the leaf gelatin and the soft-whipped cream.

Grapefruit sauce
Combine the grapefruit juice, syrup and xanthan gum.

Cherry gelatin
Combine all ingredients.

Grapefruit and Campari sorbet
Prepare some syrup with water, sugar and carob flour. Let cool and add the rest of the ingredients. Pour into the Pacojets and freeze.

Campari wafers
Combine all ingredients. Slowly pour the batter into a preheated pan on the burner, with a drizzling of sunflower seed oil to create crispy wafers.

Campari-marinated grapefruit
Supreme the grapefruit and marinate in the Campari.

Fresh fennel
Thinly slice the fennel using the mandoline and marinate in the Campari.

Presentation

Using a pastry bag, create irregular dollops of the white chocolate mousse in the center of the plate. Place the Campari-marinated grapefruit sections over the mousse and top with grapefruit sauce, fresh fennel, cherry gelatin and grapefruit and Campari sorbet and the Campari wafers.

Strawberry with caprino cheese

almond gelato and lychee and strawberry sauce

Composition

Almond cake
Almond ganache
Red glaze
Lychee and strawberry sauce
Strawberry ganache
Cheese cream
Almond gelato
Cake icing

Ingredients

Almond cake
225 g unsalted butter
25 g almond paste
125 g white sugar
125 g light brown sugar
1 g salt
150 g whole eggs
75 g cornstarch
75 g rice starch
100 g almond flour
4 g baking powder

Almond ganache
125 g heavy cream
35 g Ivoire chocolate
25 g chopped and lightly toasted almonds

Red glaze
140 g sugar
140 g water
90 g dextrose
115 g condensed milk
10 g leaf gelatin
65 g cocoa butter
140 g Absolut leaf gelatin
1 g water-soluble red food coloring

Lychee and strawberry sauce
150 g lychee purée
75 g strawberry water
500 g strawberries

Strawberry ganache
115 g unsalted butter
75 g strawberry purée
45 g whole eggs
115 g sugar
8 g cornstarch

Preparation

Almond cake
Cream the butter and sugar, add the eggs, gradually add the flours, baking powder, salt and, finally, the almond cream. Spread the mixture on a Silpat baking mat to a thickness of approx. a quarter-inch and bake in a 170°C oven for 15 minutes.

Almond ganache
The day before prepare an infusion with the cream and chopped toasted almonds. Boil the cream in a small saucepan.
Pour on the chocolate, emulsify and allow to cool, then whip in a mixer.

Red glaze
Heat the sugar, water and dextrose to 103°C.
Add the condensed milk, leaf gelatin, Absolut gelatin and, finally, the cocoa butter and food coloring.

Lychee and strawberry sauce
Place the strawberries in a bowl and cook in the microwave for 5 minutes.
Repeat to create the strawberry juice to add to the lychee purée.

Strawberry ganache
Combine the strawberry purée and butter and bring to a boil.
In the meantime, combine the rest of the ingredients, add to the purée and butter mixture and simmer until ready.

Cheese cream
Cream together all ingredients and place in a quenelle-shaped mold. Freeze and cover with the red glaze.

Almond gelato
Boil together the milk, sugar and almond flour; pour into the Pacojet beakers and freeze.

Cake icing
Melt the chocolate, add the melted cocoa butter and then the almonds.

To serve

Form the almond cake into a cup shape, using first a 7 cm pasta mold, followed by a 5 cm mold, then immerse in the chocolate icing. On top of this small cake, decorate with the almond and strawberry ganaches, add a glazed caprino cheese quenelle and complete the dish with an almond gelato quenelle on the side. Before serving, pour over the center the lychee and strawberry sauce.

Cheese cream
15 g sugar
50 g fresh caprino cheese
50 g mascarpone cheese
50 g custard

Almond gelato
1 l whole milk
200 g sugar
225 g almond flour

Cake icing
100 g Jivara milk chocolate
100 g cocoa butter
25 g chopped almonds

Pineapple

Composition

Coconut tapioca
Pineapple fondant
Coconut chips
Pineapple chips
Almond cake
Ginger gelato

Ingredients

Coconut tapioca
75 g heavy cream
250 g fresh whole milk
125 g coconut purée
125 g passion fruit purée
35 g white sugar
peel of 1/2 orange
20 g tapioca

Pineapple fondant
250 g pineapple
120 g light brown sugar
130 g glucose
200 g heavy cream
50 g milk
250 g passion fruit purée
50 g apricot purée
1 lime
2 g vanilla seeds

Coconut chips
1 coconut
200 g of sugar syrup 1:1

Pineapple chips
1/2 ananas
confectioners' sugar

Almond cake
225 g unsalted butter
25 g almond paste
125 g white sugar
1 g salt
250 g whole eggs
175 g all-purpose flour
100 g almond flour
4 g baking powder

Ginger 'gelato'
500 g fresh whole milk
25 g powdered milk
210 g heavy cream
120 g white sugar
50 g fresh ginger
18 g glucose
1 g carob flour

Preparation

Coconut tapioca
Place all ingredients in a saucepan and cook the tapioca pearls on low heat, making sure they do not stick.

Pineapple fondant
Slice the pineapple into 3/4-inch slices and place in vacuum bags together with the syrup prepared using all the other ingredients, and cook at 86°C for approx. 10 hours. Preserve the cooking liquid and trim the slices to create 4 in. x 1 in. rectangles.

Coconut chips
Slice the coconut using a mandoline slicer, place the slices in a semi sphere silicone mold with the syrup and dry them overnight at a temperature of 50°C.

Pineapple chips
Slice the pineapple with the slicer, sprinkle both sides of the slices with confectioners' sugar and dry in the oven at a temperature of 60°C-70°C for 10 hours.

Almond cake
Cream the butter and sugar, add the eggs, gradually add the flours, baking powder, salt and, finally, the almond cream. Spread the mixture on a Silpat baking mat to a thickness of approx. a quarter-inch and bake in a 170°C oven for 15 minutes.

Ginger 'gelato'
Soak the ginger in the heavy cream and milk for a day. Strain and add the rest of the ingredients. Heat to a temperature of 86°C.

Presentation

Spread the tapioca on the plate and cover with the coconut chips, the cooking liquid from the pineapple and two pineapple rectangles in the center. Next to each rectangle, place the pineapple chips and finally, a ginger gelato quenelle.

Chocolate soufflé

Composition

Chocolate Soufflé
Hibiscus and mixed berry gelatin
Raspberry gelato
Crème Chantilly with Greek yogurt and mascarpone
Rhubarb confit
Rhubarb chips
Edible flowers

Ingredients

Chocolate Soufflé

Zabaglione
- 150 g egg yolks (8 yolks)
- 50 g white sugar

Meringue
- 400 g egg whites
- 200 g white sugar

200 g 72% Araguani chocolate
200g 85% Abinao chocolate

Hibiscus and mixed berry gelatin

500 g hibiscus infusion
(500 g water, 15 g hibiscus)
230 g mixed berry purée
83 g TPT syrup
16 g leaf gelatin

Raspberry gelato

800 g milk
200 g heavy cream
50 g liquid glucose
100 g white sugar
30 g powdered milk
700 g raspberry purée

Crème Chantilly with Greek yogurt and mascarpone

50 g mascarpone cheese
150 g Greek yogurt
200 g heavy cream
1/2 vanilla bean
30 g sugar
100 g custard

Rhubarb confit

100 g rhubarb
100 g TPT syrup

Rhubarb chips

rhubarb
confectioners' sugar

Preparation

Chocolate soufflé
At the same time, prepare the zabaglione and Italian meringue, then combine them. Melt the chocolate and stir it into the meringue and zabaglione mixture.

Hibiscus and mixed berry gelatin
Combine the infusion, purée and syrup and heat to 45°C, then add the leaf gelatin.

Raspberry gelato
Combine all ingredients and blend well.

Crème Chantilly with Greek yogurt and mascarpone
Whip together the mascarpone, yogurt, cream, vanilla and sugar; add the custard.

Rhubarb confit
Bring the syrup to a boil and then remove from the heat. Cut the rhubarb into cubes and allow to seep in the syrup for about 2 hours.

Rhubarb chips
Use a mandoline to slice the rhubarb, dust both sides of the slices with confectioners' sugar and allow to dry.

Presentation

Serve the soufflé in a glass placed on a dessert plate with the mixed berry gelatin as a base and over it the crème Chantilly with Greek yogurt and mascarpone, raspberry gelato, rhubarb confit and rhubarb chips.

BY ANTONIO GUIDA

Squash

Composition

Mini squash cakes
Squash gelato
35% white chocolate mousse
Pomegranate sauce
Squash chips
Marron glacés

Ingredients

Mini squash cakes
30 g heavy cream
50 g cocoa butter
20 g unsalted butter
80 g egg whites
60 g white sugar
40 g egg yolks
200 g butternut squash purée
30 g potato flour

Squash gelato
150 g fresh whole milk
65 g white sugar
50 g egg yolks
150 g butternut squash purée
150 g heavy cream
25 g Italian meringue
coffee extract
vanilla

35% white chocolate mousse
Custard (150 g)
- 75 g heavy cream
- 75 g fresh whole milk
- 30 g egg yolks
- 15 g sugar

225 g heavy cream
300 g 35% Ivoire chocolate
3 g leaf gelatin

Pomegranate sauce
200 g pomegranate juice
50 g of sugar syrup 1:1
1 g xanthan gum

Squash chips
1 butternut squash
confectioners' sugar

Preparation

Mini squash cakes

Mix the warm squash purée with the egg yolks, melted cocoa butter and cream; whip together the egg whites and sugar until fluffy and add to the squash mixture, then add the potato flour. Spread the mixture on a Silpat baking mat to a thickness of approx. a quarter-inch and bake in a 170°C oven for 15 minutes.

Squash gelato
Prepare the custard with the milk, sugar, egg yolks, cream and squash purée. Heat to 86°C, but when the cream has reached a temperature of 38-40°C, add the meringue, coffee extract and vanilla. Freeze in the Pacojet beakers.

35% white chocolate mousse
Prepare the custard and when still warm, add the leaf gelatin and 35% Ivoire chocolate at a temperature of 35°, then fold in the soft-whipped cream.

Pomegranate sauce
Prepare the pomegranate juice in a centrifugal juicer, add the syrup and xanthan gum, then blend for a few minutes.

Squash chips
Thinly slice the squash with the slicer, creating half-moon slices. Spread the squash on a Silpat baking mat and dust with confectioners' sugar, then place in a 50°C oven for approx. 2 hours.

Presentation

Create a spiral on the plate using the white chocolate mousse. Between the curves of the spiral, add the pomegranate sauce then, in three points, place three mini squash cakes, each topped with a squash gelato quenelle and squash chips. Decorate with pomegranate and marrons glacés.

Sprouts

“They are the start of life, the freshness,
the immaturity of a flavor, color, vivacity...”

Recipe bases

Bisque

Ingredients
1 onion
1 fennel
12 vine tomatoes
lobster carcasses
7 l lobster remouillage
3 basil stems
cognac
extra virgin olive oil
sunflower seed oil

Preparation
Place a saucepan on the burner, pour in some oil, add the julienned fennel and onion and sauté until soft. Add the cubed tomatoes, then allow to cook on low heat for about 20 minutes. Remove the mixture from the heat, allow to cool and refrigerate. In a large saucepan add some sunflower seed oil and brown the lobster carcasses well. Add some cognac and allow to evaporate, moisten with some water, then add the cooked vegetable mixture. Cook for about 45 minutes, add the basil and continue cooking for an additional 15 minutes. Strain and refrigerate.

Blanquette base

Ingredients
100 g unsalted butter
100 g all-purpose flour
100 g heavy cream
1 l stock

Preparation
Combine all ingredients and cook in the oven at 165°C for approx. 45 minutes.

Chicken mousseline

Ingredients
for 210 g mousseline
130 g chicken breast
80 g cream
12 g salt

Preparation
Place the chicken breast in the Robot Coupe, blend, add the salt and finally the cream.

Sour butter

Ingredients
1/2 l white wine vinegar
375 g white wine
5 Sarawak peppercorns
1 bay leaves
1/2 onion
1 tarragon sprig
500 g butter

Preparation
Cut the butter into pieces, place in a bowl and work at room temperature until soft. Place all the other ingredients in a small saucepan and reduce by 30%, then pass through a chinois and add the mixture to the butter. Refrigerate.

Suprême sauce

Ingredients
reduced chicken stock
reduced cream
foie gras
white porto
cognac

Preparation
Combine all ingredients, bring to the boil and blend. Salt and pepper to taste. Strain.

The team and Seta

Center of Milan. Hotel Mandarin Oriental. First you cross through the foyer. The interiors are the work of architect Antonio Citterio. Then, there it is: Seta. The restaurant's decor is elegant and sophisticated, with velvet upholstery in a contemporary color scheme of dark teal, beige and dusty rose. The lighting is soft and the acoustics perfect. It looks out on the courtyard, where urban denizens enjoy an aperitif or sit at the bistro tables when the weather is clement. The venue unfolds gradually before us. Next to Seta is another outdoor space for guests from spring into the warmer months. This is the physical space that made Antonio Guida's cuisine famous, following his scintillating years at the Pellicano Hotel in Porto Ercole in Tuscany. As we make our way towards the kitchen, we are met with smiles, enthusiasm, freshness and youth. "Our work is hard, the hours are demanding. It is important to support my team, to help them and listen to them so they can grow. I try to exert my authority gently and make people who work with me serene and aware, so they love what they do." In Antonio Guida's kitchen there is always an aroma of food and a serious and enthusiastic team. "My mother taught me this, an excellent cook and organizer who, from the time we were small, assigned each of us a different task based on our various abilities." Here, there is no bad language or rude behavior. There is no tension, except that generated by intense concentration and the desire to do everything perfectly. "Mistakes can be corrected. Of course, they need to be in good faith, and in most cases they are. In fact, the turnover in my kitchen is very low." Federico Dell'Omarino, Antonio's right-hand man and Seta's executive sous chef, leads the team members every day and is jokingly referred to as the group's "psychologist". He and Antonio met in Rome and Federico followed him. Antonio without Federico, or Federico without Antonio just don't exist. "Chef Guida has given me everything, the chance to make it to haute cuisine. He's a real friend, almost a relative!" adds Dell'Omarino. He manages the team in an easy and friendly way, while Antonio is quieter. To everyone's amazement, he and the chef sometimes clean the fish together, like budding apprentices. "It's a simple way of teaching that you can never stop getting your hands dirty and that even the most menial task is important—invaluable—in achieving our goals," he says. Nicola Di Lena is Seta's pastry chef. With a mother from Sicilia and father from Apulia, he is the third member of Antonio's team, his "dream team". The chef, "Fede" and Nicola are like the three musketeers, "all-for-one-and-one-for-all"—friends who are always ready to joke and make fun of each other, like real brothers. "My dream was always to become a pastry chef and I grew up watching my mother make custard, stirring it with half a lemon stuck on a fork. As she stirred and stirred, the aroma became stronger and filled the kitchen. We lived in Switzerland because my parents had emigrated there for work. Meeting Chef Guida changed my life. One of the paths of life that leads you to an unexpected destination. Antonio gave me the opportunity to improve. I learned to reduce the amount of sugar and to add more butter and this made my pastry style lighter and more sophisticated." Antonio contact-

Antonio, Federico Dell'Omarino and the dining room team

ed Nicola while he was at the Posta Vecchia, the twin hotel of the Pellicano. "It was an encounter that changed my destiny. I took the train, he came to get me at the station and we went to the kitchen. I was a kid. I had always worked on cruise ships. I had traveled the Mediterranean and I knew what hard work and organization meant, but there was no way I was up to the level of a starred restaurant." As he talks, his eyes begin to glisten and he clenches his hands to overcome his shyness. His demeanor is simple and polite. "Antonio absolutely loved desserts, so I was with an expert. Plus, he had been in a major French kitchen, Monsieur Gagnaire's. He asked me about how I worked, what my background was. I got my start in Matera and in my uncle's pastry shop in Sicily, working there first on the weekends and in the summer when the hotel and catering school was out. It was a world of cassate, cannoncini, candied fruit and babà." He stayed the first season when Ivan Le Pape was at the Pellicano, and he was the first to arrive and the last to leave. The kid had what it took and he worked hard. And his pastry style blossomed like roses in the spring. Working with Laurent Jeannin at the Epicure (3 Michelin stars) in Paris completed his training. Nicola had met Antonio, Antonio had met Nicola. In fact, between them, the traditional divide between chef and pastry chef typical of many kitchens does not exist at Seta. Nicola knows all the dishes and can substitute Guida and Dell'Omarino if necessary. People eating at the chef's table will see Nicola leading the team with an effective, self-possessed ease, in pure Guida style. Dushan Warnakulasuriya, whom everyone calls Duscian, comes from Sri Lanka and is the antipasto and first course sous chef. While studying economics at university, he left his homeland to escape the civil war. Arrived in Italy, he washed dishes in an Italian deli in Varese in order to send money back home, and in the kitchen of a Sicilian chef. Then the course at the Culinary Institute for foreigners in Castiglione d'Asti changed his life and meeting Antonio was the decisive turn. His eyes, somewhat melancholy, are those of someone who has worked hard, but he always has a broad smile on his face, even when very tired. "At a certain point, I was working in a restaurant at night and in a gelateria during the day. By mid-morning, I had to have finished 62 flavors!". Then the encounter with Chef Guida (whom he always refers to this way, as if the words were fused together), winters in St. Hubertus at the Rosa Alpina, recommended to Norbert Niederkofler by Antonio, and summers at the Pellicano until the move to Milan where he became one of the main players. Behind the service pass is Luigi Oliviero, from Naples, who spent an extended period in restaurants in London, including with Gordon Ramsay, at Clardige's and the Dorchester Hotel, finishing for a while in Melbourne, Australia. Then Milan. "Our chef explains the overall picture to us, the general perspective. We don't only talk about the individual dishes. And he trusts us because he says that since we have repeated the same dish many more times than he has, we know how to do it well."

Directing the Seta dining room is Manuel Tempesta, a native of Padua who has worked at the Savoy in London. "The dining room is a world of its own. You have to make decisions in the blink of an eye and we work well together. We are a team," he adds. With Manuel is sommelier Andrea Aloi from Trento. A chessmaster at age 26, he worked in a bank. But then, "wine called", as he says. "I drank my first (exceptional) glass with a friend whom I was teaching to play. And between a king and a queen, he offered me a Clos des Mouches. It was a revelation. Then I decided at the Worldsom School in Bordeaux where they also teach how to taste water, tea, coffee and wines. I've only been at Seta for a short time, but I've learned more from Chef Guida than in the rest of my life. He even has those of us who work in the dining room taste a lot, in order to refresh our memories, to be more convincing in our explanations and, in my case, to create the best rapport between wine and food."

Seta, Mandarin Oriental, Milan

Luca Finardi, Area Vice President, Operations
and General Manager of Mandarin Oriental, Milan

Antonio with Federico Dell'Omarino,
Nicola Di Lena, pastry chef,
and Manuel Tempesta, dining room
manager in the Seta dehors

Manuel Tempesta, Luis Diaz, Gianluca De Marco, Andrea Loi

Romina Ridolfi, chef de rang at Seta

Federico Paolella, maître assistant at Seta

I would like to thank Maddalena and Giacomo with whom I shared so many wonderful moments in writing this book; Federico Dell'Omarino and Nicola Di Lena, as always at my side; the marvelous team from Seta who, daily, give their all; and Manuel Tempesta and Andrea Loi managing the floor. Special thanks go to Dr Giuseppe Statuto and Luca Finardi, who have supported me with their enthusiasm and expertise during this project with the Mandarin Oriental, Milan.
And thanks to Romano who, with me, wrote that plan in the notebook; chef Pantaleo who gave me such invaluable advice; Rafelino Bello and the fundamental values he communicated to me; and chef Pierre Gagnaire, a true human being and not just a tremendously talented chef who changed my life. I cannot forget Stefano Baiocco; my close friends Gianfranco Pannettone, Andrea Giacomobono, Stefano Casalena, Renato Viola, Hervé Nepple, Francisco Bouza, Marie Soria; the Sciò family who gave me such an important opportunity; and Cinzia Fanciulli and Gianni Alocci.
And, of course, my dear friends in Depressa and my family, in particular my mom and dad who have always been there for me.
And thanks to Luciana and Viola, my girls, who provide steadfast support in this crazy journey of mine.

Silvana Editoriale

Direction
Dario Cimorelli

Art Director
Giacomo Merli

Editorial Coordinator
Sergio Di Stefano

Copy Editor
Clelia Valentina Palmese

Production Coordinator
Antonio Micelli

Editorial Assistant
Ondina Granato

Photo Editor
Alessandra Olivari, Silvia Sala

Press Office
Lidia Masolini, press@silvanaeditoriale.it

Prepress
Eric Guglielmi

Silvana Editoriale S.p.A.
via dei Lavoratori, 78
20092 Cinisello Balsamo, Milano
tel. 02 453 951 01
fax 02 453 951 51
www.silvanaeditoriale.it

Reproductions, printing and binding in Italy
Printed by Faenza Group S.p.A.
Printed in February 2020

FSC
www.fsc.org
MIX
Paper from
responsible sources
FSC® C020465